WORLD WAR II

ANDREW McNEIL

Acknowledgements
We wish to thank the following
organizations for their assistance and for making
available material in their collections.
Imperial War Museum
Robert Hunt Library
U.S. Signal Corps
'Beach-head' and 'Carrier'
devised by Citadel Boardgames Ltd.

Illustrators
Paul Buckle
Gordon C. Davies
Terry Hadler
Brian Lewis
Michael Roffe

Art and editorial direction
David Jefferis
Rules editor
James Opie
Text editors
Tony Allan
Margaret Chester
Picture researchers
Caroline Lucas
Ann Davies
Typesetting
Diagraphic, London. Trade Spools, Frome, Somerset
Colour reproduction
Reproduction Colour Services, Pudsey, Yorkshire

Made and printed in Great Britain

© 1975 Usborne Publishing Ltd

All rights reserved. No part of this publication
may be reproduced, stored in a retrieval system
or transmitted in any form or by any means,
electronic, mechanical, photocopying, recording
or otherwise, without the prior permission of
the publisher.

First published in 1975 by
Usborne Publishing Ltd
20 Garrick Street
London WC2E 9BH

First published in paperback
in 1983.

The Italian Beretta Model 1934 pistol was used by the Italian Army throughout World War 2. The magazine held seven rounds and slotted into the pistol's butt.

The British Bren light machine-gun was a tough and reliable weapon. The gun was designed in Czechoslovakia, but was developed and produced in England. The magazine held 30 rounds of ammunition.

ABOUT THIS BOOK

World War 2 is a war book with a difference. It tells you what happened in the war, and also includes four new boardgames, complete with rules and cut-out pieces, based on real wartime situations.

It gives a balanced picture of a world in conflict, covering the bitter fighting between Germany and Russia as well as the Battle of Britain, and the island war in the Pacific as well as the struggle for the Atlantic shipping routes.

The games are just as varied. In 'Carrier,' American and Japanese fleets clash in the Pacific. 'Winter War' pits German invasion forces against the Red Army deep in Russia. In 'Air Assault', German fighters try to stop Allied planes from bombing targets in occupied France. 'Beach-head' is based on the D-Day landings, and features the 'funnies' – special-purpose tanks designed to beat the shore defences.

CONTENTS

4	Blitzkrieg
6	On the Russian front
8	Pacific war
10	Battle of the Atlantic
12	Thrust into Europe
15	Defeat of Japan
16	Timechart
	Improving and storing game pieces
17	Rules and cut-out pieces for four battlegames
25	Supplying the front line
26	Battlegame 1 – Winter War
28	'Flat-tops' in the Pacific
30	Battlegame 2 – Carrier
32	Air war over Europe
34	Battlegame 3 – Air Assault
36	Clearing the beaches
38	Battlegame 4 – Beach-head

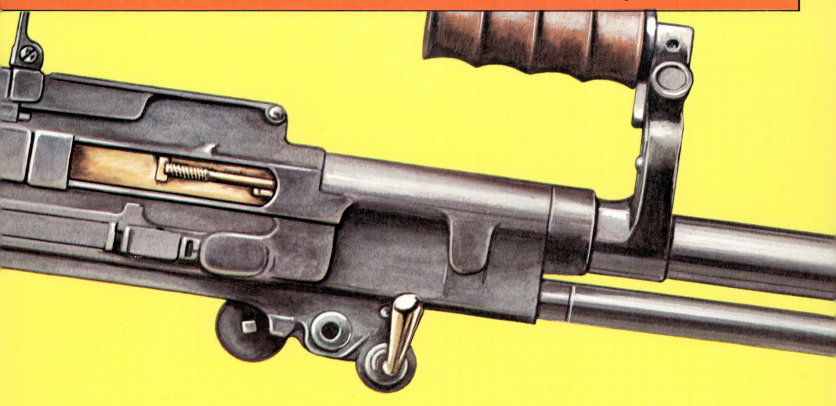

BLITZKRIEG

World War 2 began in 1939. But the reasons for it went back twenty years, to the end of World War 1. In that war Germany and Austria-Hungary were beaten by the Allies. But ten million men had been killed. Twenty million were wounded. People said there must be no more wars.

Unhappily the Allies thought the best way to prevent war was to punish the Germans. The harsh peace terms made Germany very poor and hard to govern, and its people very bitter. The Germans turned to the Nazis, who said they would make the country great again.

Hitler seizes power

The Nazi Party gained control under Hitler in 1933. Germany was rearmed, although the peace terms forbade this. By 1939 her army and air force (the Luftwaffe) were the strongest in the world.

On September 1 the Germans invaded Poland, and conquered her in three weeks, using a new type of warfare. This was 'blitzkrieg', or lightning war. Dive-bombers smashed troops and planes on the ground. Meanwhile mechanized troops, with tanks, moved quickly forwards, encircling and capturing men and material.

The war begins

Britain and France had let Hitler take Austria and Czechoslovakia without fighting. But the attack on Poland made them declare war on Germany, on September 3, 1939. World War 2 had begun.

In 1940 the Germans quickly conquered Denmark and Norway, and then struck west, invading Holland and Belgium on May 10.

The blitzkrieg worked again. German armoured columns broke through the French lines in a few days. They then raced to cut off the Allied troops in Holland and Belgium. On May 14 Holland surrendered, and Belgium two weeks later. The British army was evacuated from Dunkirk. But it lost most of its equipment.

The French lost a third of their strength in the battle for the Low Countries, but they went on fighting for another three weeks. When they surrendered on June 22, only Britain remained in the fight.

The Battle of Britain

The Germans now turned to attacking Britain by air. The Battle of Britain was fought from July to September. The British had fewer aircraft than the Germans but their planes were better.

▲ **In the early years** of the war, the Germans only used light tanks like the PzKw II shown in camouflage above. They relied on speed rather than on heavy armament to sweep their troops to victory. The infantry kept up with the tanks on motor-cycles and in armoured half-tracked vehicles.

The Luftwaffe also made a bad mistake. It switched its attack to London, instead of going on bombing R.A.F. fighter bases and radar stations. The attacks on London caused great damage and loss of life. But they didn't help the Germans' plans to invade Britain. By the middle of September they had failed to gain control of the air and had to give up these plans.

Into Russia

In 1941 the whole face of the war changed. After a blitzkrieg campaign in Greece, and a paratroop invasion of Crete, the Germans attacked the Soviet Union on June 22, 1941. It was the greatest land invasion in history – the supreme test of blitzkrieg warfare.

▲**On September 1, 1939,** five German armies invaded Poland. Using blitzkrieg tactics, they soon defeated the smaller Polish forces. Russia took part of eastern Poland.

▲**After seizing** neutral Denmark and Norway, the Germans attacked in the west in May 1940. Badly led but fighting bravely, the French and British were beaten in five weeks.

▲**In April 1941,** the Germans invaded Greece and Yugoslavia. Rapid advances and an airborne landing in Crete brought them victory within a few weeks.

The terror tactics of lightning war

Air and ground forces worked together in the blitzkrieg ('lightning war') campaigns. The enemy air force was the first target. It was put out of action as soon as possible by bombing and machine-gunning airfields.

Freed from enemy air interference, German bombers and fighters were then able to make the fast-moving ground forces' job easier by attacking enemy troops as they moved up to the front. Road and rail bridges were not bombed because the Germans needed to use them for their advance.

The tanks and motorized forces moved forward as quickly as possible. The tanks advanced in a wedge formation to punch a hole in the enemy lines. The motorized infantry then kept the gap open while more tanks dashed through and fanned outwards on the other side. Others pushed on far behind the enemy lines. The tanks did not stop to defeat all enemy forces. That job was left to the infantry and artillery following them. Parachute and glider troops also landed behind the lines to add to the problems of the enemy generals.

The enemy were generally so confused by these tactics that they were unable to mount counter-attacks until it was too late. They were surrounded and forced to surrender.

ON THE RUSSIAN FRONT

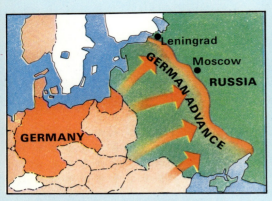

▲**Russia's vast size** proved too much for the German armies, and they failed to reach their main objectives – including Moscow.

Eight days before they invaded Poland the Germans made an agreement with Russia. Russia agreed to let Germany take half of Poland. Russia was to take the other half. It was a wicked agreement. But it did not last, because Nazi Germany and communist Russia hated and feared each other.

The Soviet Union is a huge country. The Germans used a huge army to try to conquer it. At first their blitzkrieg tactics worked well. Hundreds of thousands of Russians were killed or captured. Over 3,000 tanks and 4,000 planes were lost.

The blitzkrieg fails

When winter stopped them the Germans had reached Odessa on the Black Sea. In the north Leningrad was under siege. In the centre they were a few miles from Moscow. They held 500,000 square miles of Russia. But their blitzkrieg had failed. They had not won the lightning victory they needed.

The Russians suffered terrible losses in the first six months. But they survived. Now, from behind the Ural Mountains, from factories out of reach of German bombers, came new tanks, guns and planes. Two new tanks, the T-34 and the KV-1, proved to be better than the Germans'.

The Germans' equipment was worn out after two years of war. The Russian winter also took a heavy toll. Russian tanks had auxiliary engines to start them in the intense cold. German tanks had to be warmed up by blow-torches. The Russians were used to fighting in winter. The Germans were not equipped for it.

For more than two years Europe's two largest nations fought each other, in battles that covered hundreds of miles and lasted many weeks. The fighting was some of the hardest the world has seen.

Tank warfare

The most important weapon was the tank. The Germans used the same tanks as they had in the west. These were mainly PzKw IIIs and PzKw IVs. But the heavier and better-armed PzKw IV was gradually becoming their main battle-tank. (PzKw is short for *Panzerkampfwagen*, the German word for tank.) The tanks were backed up by infantry in armoured half-tracks or lorries.

The eyes of the Panzer (armoured) Division were the armoured cars and half-tracks of the reconnaissance battalion. Heavier support was given by

The tank that blunted the German advance

The Russians had long known how important tanks would be in modern warfare, and when the Germans invaded in 1941 they had just perfected a medium tank, the T-34, that was better than anything the Germans had. It was fast, well-armoured and reliable. Its design was simple enough for it to be produced in large numbers.

Forty thousand T-34s were made, half of them with powerful 85 mm guns that could outfire the Germans. The T-34 was probably the most successful tank produced during the war.

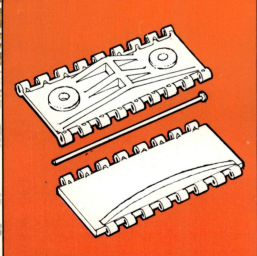

▲**Tracks are an important part** of a tank. They have to stand up to rough treatment. On T-34s, a pin joined the plates, its head next to the hull. It was pushed back into place by a sloped plate if it worked loose.

Few Russian tanks had radios till late in the war, and even then they were inefficient. American radios and parts were sometimes used.

This G.M.C. truck was one of thousands sent to Russia from the U.S.A. They kept supplies moving, and played a vital part when the Russian offensives began.

Good suspension and wide tracks gave the tanks a cross-country speed of 25 m.p.h. When there was no more rubber to make tyres, steel wheels without tyres were used instead.

The armour was sloped in front so that shots glanced off it. Only three thicknesses of armour were used, the thickest in the turret. The tank carried 77 rounds of ammunition.

▲ **The steppes** of Russia's Ukraine were ideal country for tanks, and the Germans made rapid advances in the summers of 1941 and 1942. But in winter it was a different matter. Bitter cold froze men to death, and planes and tanks could not move.

assault guns (like tanks without turrets) and heavy mortars and 88 mm guns.

Tigers and Panthers

The Russian T-34 and KV-1 tanks were more than a match for the PzKw Vs. The T-34 was produced in huge numbers. It moved very fast and had a big gun. The Germans had to design another tank to try to beat it. This was the PzKw V, called the Panther. An even larger tank, the biggest to be made in large numbers in the war, was the PzKw VI, or Tiger.

The Russians couldn't match the German artillery, armoured cars or assault guns. But they could produce huge amounts of what they needed, and used it to good effect. It was by their greater production that the Soviet Union won the war on the Eastern Front.

The war in the air

The Russians also had some superb planes to support their ground troops. Their Ilyushin Il 2, called the Stormovik, caused havoc among the German tanks. And their Yak 9 was an effective fighter and fighter-bomber. The Germans relied on the Stuka and then on 'tank-busting' planes like the Henschel Hs 129. As fighters they used the Messerschmitt 109 and Focke-Wulf 190.

The war in Russia fell into two phases. Until the middle of 1943 the Germans were on the offensive. Then, after fighting fiercely for the industrial basin of the Don and Volga, they were defeated at Stalingrad. There 300,000 Germans were killed or captured. It was the German Army's first defeat.

The turn of the tide

In the summer of 1943 the Germans were defeated at Kursk, in the biggest tank battle in history. Within days the Russians took up the offensive. Two years later they entered Berlin.

The 76 mm gun could beat German tanks. When the Germans increased their tanks' fire-power, the T-34 was given thicker armour and a more powerful 85 mm gun.

The crew of four was led by the tank commander, who also fired the gun. The other members were the loader, the driver, and the co-driver, who worked the hull machine-gun and acted as mechanic as well.

The low turret gave good protection, but made it difficult to lower the gun. Visibility for the commander was poor at first, but was improved in later models.

The 12-cylinder diesel engine was sturdy and reliable. It was started by a small compressed-air engine, vital in the Russian winter.

PACIFIC WAR

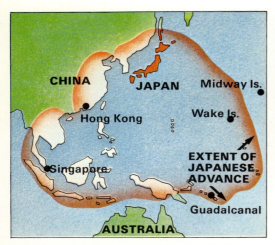

▲**Unprepared for Japanese superiority** in ships and planes, and taken by surprise, U.S., British and Dutch forces were soon overrun.

In World War 1 Japan fought on the side of the Allies. Afterwards she felt they had treated her badly. She had become Asia's first industrial nation. But she felt restricted by American and British interests. Above all, she needed raw materials, like oil and rubber. So she went to war to get them; first against China, weakened by civil war, in 1937, and then in 1941 against the United States and Britain.

The bombing of Pearl Harbour

On December 7, 1941, without any declaration of war, 360 carrier-borne Japanese aircraft attacked Pearl Harbour, the American naval base in Hawaii. Four U.S. battleships were sunk and another four damaged; 247 planes were destroyed.

At the same time Japanese forces attacked American bases in the Philippines, and the British in Hong Kong. Hong Kong fell in less than three weeks. In the Philippines the last American and Filipino units surrendered in May 1942.

Singapore falls

The Japanese also invaded Malaya. This was their biggest operation. In two months they had pushed the British, Australian and Indian troops back to Singapore. In one of the greatest defeats ever suffered by the British, Singapore itself surrendered on February 15, 1942. By mid-May Japan controlled South East Asia and the western Pacific from the Indian border in the west to Wake Island in the east.

Japan's success was largely due to the skill and spirit of her troops. Japanese soldiers were very good at jungle warfare. They could march many miles a day in conditions intolerable to Europeans. There were very few roads in the Malay Peninsula but the Japanese did not need them as they used two-wheel carts and bicycles, rather than motor transport.

Though they were badly equipped by Western standards, the Japanese had a deep pride in their country and would die rather than surrender. They had been ruled by soldiers for more than ten years. And since they had been fighting China since 1937 their troops were experienced and well trained.

Carrier war

They also mastered a new type of warfare, dominated by aircraft-carriers and the planes they carried. The Japanese built the first ship specially designed to carry aircraft. Their carriers were superb, and the planes that took off from them were better than any the Allies had at the beginning of the Pacific War.

To attack the enemy's big ships there was the Nakajima B5N, a torpedo-bomber, nicknamed Kate by the Allies. To attack both sea and land targets there was the Aichi D3A, a dive-bomber (nicknamed Val). To protect these planes from enemy fighters there was the Mitsubishi Zero fighter, a highly manoeuvrable plane. All three were fast and had the great range necessary in so large an area.

Bomber support

Japan's land-based planes played a big part too. In the Malayan campaign bombers supported the troops from bases in Indo-China. As the Japanese seized more islands in the Indies and Pacific they captured or built more bases. From these they flew medium bombers.

The Japanese conquered a vast area

▲**Without declaring war,** the Japanese attacked the U.S. naval base at Pearl Harbour in Hawaii. This surprise attack knocked out the Pacific Fleet, except for the vital aircraft-carriers, but made the Americans determined to win a war started so treacherously.

very quickly. They bombed as far afield as Darwin in Australia and Colombo in Ceylon. It was inevitable that in the end they would extend themselves too far.

Things began to go less smoothly in April 1942. A Japanese force moved to attack Port Moresby on New Guinea, the last Allied foothold north of Australia. In the Battle of the Coral Sea, U.S. carrier-borne planes sank a Japanese carrier and damaged another. The Americans lost one carrier. But the Japanese advance was halted.

The Americans had recovered quickly from Pearl Harbour and the loss of so many bases. Their two Pacific-based carriers were away from Hawaii when Pearl Harbour was bombed. And though their planes, like the Douglas Devastator and Dauntless, were not so advanced as those of the Japanese, they were very effective in the hands of their skilled pilots. It was the Dauntless that at first did most damage to the Japanese.

The Battle of Midway

In June 1942 the Japanese tried to knock out the American base of Midway in the central Pacific. They were heavily defeated. Four Japanese carriers were sunk, in a much bigger battle than that in the Coral Sea. It was one of the turning-points of the war. After the Battle of Midway Japan had no hope of defeating the vast power and resources of the United States.

JUNGLE WARFARE

▼**The Japanese soldier** fought with great bravery and no thought for his own life. He could march many miles a day through difficult country on little food. He was generally equipped with a rifle designed as long ago as 1905, but his supporting machine-guns and mortars were fine weapons for jungle fighting.

▼**Soldiers of the Netherlands** East Indies Army, both Dutch and Indonesian, had trained to defend the heavily-populated islands of the archipelago. But weakened by the German occupation of the Dutch homeland in 1940, they were no match for the more numerous soldiers of imperial Japan.

▲**The soldiers of the Indian Army** fought the Japanese in Burma and Malaya and within the borders of India. They were among the best-trained soldiers of the war. Their equipment was the same as that of the British Army—well-tried and reliable machine-guns and mortars. They included regiments of Gurkhas, the fierce fighters from mountainous Nepal.

▲**The American soldier** was the best equipped. The M1 automatic rifle, Thompson submachine-gun, and Browning heavy machine-gun provided him with plenty of fire-power. He was backed up by good air support and efficient planning behind the lines. But at Guadalcanal, Tarawa and Iwo Jima, U.S. Marines—'Leathernecks'—faced some of the war's toughest fighting.

BATTLE OF THE ATLANTIC

In World War 1 German submarines nearly defeated Britain by sinking the ships bringing her food and raw materials. In World War 2 Germany tried even harder to cut Britain's vital supply lines.

The mighty German Navy

The German Navy of 1939 was designed for the job. It had several battleships, battle cruisers and cruisers, and more than 100 submarines (U-boats). Aircraft of the Luftwaffe acted as eyes for the ships and also attacked on their own.

The battle between these forces and those of Britain and the United States is known as the Battle of the Atlantic.

In the first two years the Germans did well. The British had too few warships to protect their shipping and too few planes to drive off the Heinkel, Dornier and Focke-Wulf Condor bombers. In 1940 and 1941 they lost more ships than they could replace, even with American help. And Germany was building about 15 U-boats a month – far more than the British could sink.

The sinking of the 'Bismarck'

Only against surface ships did the British do well. The pocket battleship *Graf Spee* was scuttled in December 1939 after being damaged by British cruisers in the south Atlantic. In May 1941 Germany's finest battleship, the *Bismarck*, was sunk – after sinking Britain's own finest battleship, the *Hood*.

Germany had led the world in U-boat development, as World War 1 had shown. She was still ahead when World War 2 started.

Most U-boats had a limited range and had to be supplied at sea. Submarines called 'milch-cows' carried fuel and supplies from U-boat bases in France and met the smaller submarines in mid-ocean. Surface ships also supplied U-boats, but they were easier to attack.

Allied losses rise

After America came into the war Allied shipping losses rose even higher. Hundreds of British and American ships were sunk in the Atlantic. In May 1942 the Allies lost 91 ships, totalling 452,000 tons. Then suddenly things began to improve.

The Allies had realized that to beat the U-boats R.A.F. Coastal Command had to have more aircraft, with the latest sort of radar to find and surprise the U-boats on the surface. Gradually more planes and better equipment were provided. More important still, the crews of the planes became more experienced.

Even then the Germans did better for a time, by changing their tactics and using

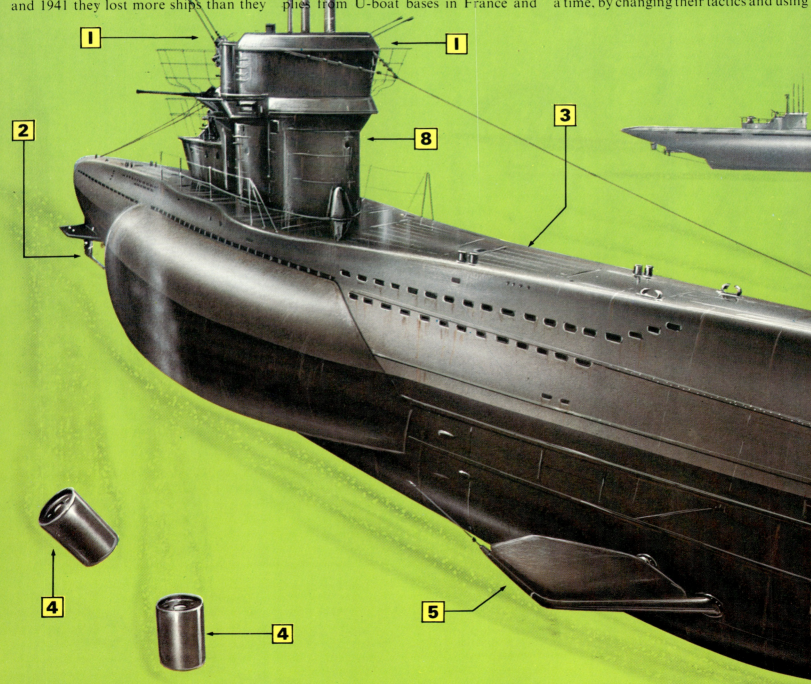

a new weapon. Their U-boats were fitted with powerful anti-aircraft guns and ordered to fight back on the surface once they were discovered. They managed to do well in gun battles with the aircraft, which had to fly in close to drop their bombs or fire their rockets.

The Germans also introduced the acoustic torpedo, which was attracted by the sound of an escort vessel's propellers. A U-boat could disable the escort and then sink the unprotected convoy with its ordinary torpedoes. The Allies were lucky to find ways of dealing with this weapon fairly quickly.

The escort system

By the middle of 1943 the Germans were forced to admit defeat in the Atlantic. More and more aircraft were being used to protect the shipping routes. And convoys of merchant ships now had better naval protection too.

This protection was in three parts. There was the usual close escort of destroyers, corvettes and other small craft. And now the Allies had enough ships to provide a support group too, to be put in where it was most needed. In addition there were the escort carriers, from which aircraft could guard the waters farther out.

Defeating the U-boats

The defeat of the U-boats in the Atlantic was vitally important to the Allies. They could have seriously hampered the preparations for invading occupied Europe. Earlier they could have knocked Britain out of the war, by starving her of the supplies she needed from across the Atlantic.

The Germans built 1,162 U-boats during the war. They sank a total of 2,828 ships, totalling more than 14 million tons. But the Allies sank 785 U-boats, with aircraft accounting for a greater proportion than surface ships. The Battle of the Atlantic was fought between small groups of men and machines over the biggest battlefield of the war.

Ways of fighting the underwater menace

▲**Aircraft of all types** were the most successful weapons against U-boats on the surface. Rockets took a heavy toll later in the war.

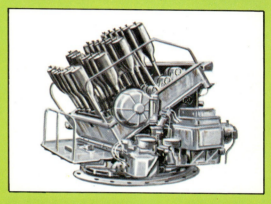

▲**The Hedgehog** could fire 24 mortar bombs in a pattern ahead of the attacking ship. The bombs would explode on contact with a U-boat.

▲**Depth charges** only needed a near miss to force a U-boat to the surface. The Allies steadily improved them during the course of the war.

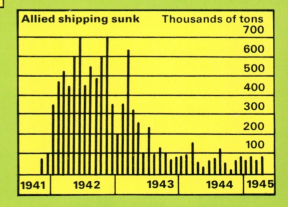

▲**As methods of attack improved,** the vital balance between tonnage of shipping lost and U-boats sunk tipped in the Allies' favour.

The Type VII U-boat

1. **Anti-aircraft guns** became more powerful as the war went on. This U-boat carried four of them.
2. **A propeller** drove the submarine along at the good speed of 17 knots on the surface. Underwater its speed was 7 knots.
3. **The hull** was 218 feet long. This U-boat weighed 769 tons.
4. **Depth charges** could crack the hull and force the boat to surface even without a direct hit.
5. **Hydroplanes** control a submarine when it surfaces and dives.
6. **Torpedoes** were efficient weapons against merchantmen, which had no defences against them.
7. **Firing tubes.** There were five of these in the Type VII model, one of them in the stern. It carried 14 torpedoes.
8. **The conning-tower** was the 'bridge' of the U-boat when it was on the surface.
9. **Refuelling submarines** known as 'milch-cows' were used to service the other U-boats.

THRUST INTO EUROPE

▲ **The tide turned** against Hitler after German defeats in North Africa and Russia. In 1943-44 the Allies threw a noose around occupied Europe, and after D-Day they tightened it on Germany.

▲ **The Russians** went on the offensive after Kursk in July 1943. They now had more tanks, guns and planes than the Germans, and they pushed forward on a thousand-mile front.

▲ **British and American troops** landed in Sicily from North Africa in July and captured the island in a rapid campaign. But the German and Italian defenders were allowed to withdraw to

▲ **In eastern Europe** the Russians kept the German armies on the move, never allowing them to dig in for defence. Only on the River Vistula (above) in Poland could the Germans make a stand. In August 1944, the Germans lost Rumania, their major source of oil and grain.

▲ **German scientists** led by rocket pioneer Wernher von Braun had developed the V (Vengeance) weapons by 1944. The V-2 (shown here) was powerful but unreliable. Of the 4,000 V-2s launched at targets in Britain, fewer than 1,500 reached their destination.

The surrender of the German 6th Army at Stalingrad in 1943 was the turning point of the war in Europe. For nearly two of its three years, the Russians had borne the brunt of the fighting. They now waited for their allies to open a second front, in the west. It seemed that with the Germans fighting on two fronts the Allies would win very quickly. In fact, for many reasons, it took them until May 1945.

The Allies' mistake

The Allies made one big mistake. They thought they could beat the Germans by bombing their factories. Every night R.A.F. bombers flew from England to bomb Germany. By day U.S.A.F. bombers did the same. Hundreds of planes were shot down. Thousands of airmen died. Much of the Allied war effort went in replacing them.

But German industry could not be destroyed from the air. By 1944, after two years of large-scale bombing, the Germans were producing five times as many fighters and three times as many tanks as in 1942.

In August 1942 the Allies made a large-scale raid on the French coast at Dieppe, and suffered heavy losses. This made them think that an attack on the coast of France could not succeed without a vast invasion force. Above all they needed thousands of landing craft. It would take more than a year to build these and train the troops to go in them.

The North African campaign

The Allies were also fighting in the south, first in North Africa and then in Sicily and Italy. The North African campaign started in 1941. It was important because it kept the Mediterranean in Allied hands.

The German Afrika Korps, under Rommel, was sent to help the Italian armies in Libya. Rommel was a brilliant general and gave the Allies a difficult time until he was finally driven back at El Alamein in October 1942. The Germans and Italians went on fighting the Allies in North Africa until May 1943.

From North Africa the Allies crossed to Sicily – on July 10, 1943. They captured the island in five weeks. The Italians had always been half-hearted allies of the Germans. After the capture of Sicily they asked the Allies for an armistice. At this, the Germans quickly rushed in their own troops to occupy Italy.

The Germans in Italy

Italy is an easy country to defend because it is so mountainous. The Germans were good soldiers, led by a good general, Kesselring. And they were well equipped, with heavy mortars and anti-

Italy. Although the Italians surrendered, the Germans defended every mile of the rough and mountainous Italian peninsula. The campaign was a failure as a second front against Germany.

▲**After two years of preparation** the Allies landed in Normandy on June 6, 1944 – D-Day. The landings, helped by specially adapted tanks, were a complete success. But in the campaign that followed the Germans put up stiff resistance before being pushed back to the borders of Germany and their fortified 'Westwall'. Allied air supremacy hastened the German retreat.

▲ **In December 1944** German tanks launched a counter-attack in the Ardennes hills on the border of France and Belgium. After early successes, the attack failed for lack of petrol.

▲**The last barrier** for the Allies in the west was the River Rhine. Helped by finding a bridge intact, the Allies launched a 'mini-D-Day' assault, crossing the river in March 1945.

▲ **The last major battle** of the war was for the German capital, Berlin. As Russian troops entered the city, the Reichstag government building caught fire and Hitler committed suicide.

tank guns. So the Allied advance was very slow and wasteful of men. And as a second front it was useless.

The real second front was opened on June 6, 1944 (D-Day), with the invasion of Normandy. It was the largest amphibious invasion in history. The Allied armies secured five beach-heads and began a long battle with the Germans in France.

The battle for Normandy lasted five weeks. The Germans tried to contain the invaders in Normandy and the Cherbourg peninsula, while the Allies tried to break out. Some of the fiercest fighting was round the town of Caen, which was the key to the left (eastern) flank of the Allied army.

Breakthrough at St. Lô

The Americans eventually broke through at St. Lô. They then threatened to encircle the Germans with a determined armoured thrust. A great many Germans escaped from the trap but they lost a lot of heavy equipment. They were now forced to draw back to the German border.

The Germans couldn't hold out on two fronts for long. They made many counter-attacks, but could only slow up the Allies for a few weeks at a time. Their largest counter-attack was in the wooded area of the Ardennes, in winter. Known as the Battle of the Bulge, it was a fine example of the effective use of armour.

The Germans failed because they had no control of the air. They only succeeded in using up their armoured reserve. They couldn't stop the Allies from crossing the Rhine, Germany's last defensive barrier, in March 1945.

In the east the Russians had to clear the Germans from a much bigger area. But they had more men and increasingly better equipment than the Germans and they pushed them back steadily. It was now impossible for the Germans to win the war.

Battle for Berlin

In January the Russians entered Germany from the east and pushed towards Berlin. The battle for the city began on April 16 and ended after fierce fighting on May 2. Hitler, the German leader, killed himself. A few days earlier, farther south, American and Russian troops had joined up. On May 8, 1945, the war in Europe ended with the unconditional surrender of the German forces.

The war left much of Europe in ruins. Millions of people had died. Among them were at least 5 million Jews and 15 million other European civilians murdered by the Nazis. More than 3 million Germans and twice as many Russians had died in battle.

Last-ditch defenders

The Messerschmitt 163A rocket fighter (left) was one product of German technical genius that reached the production stage. Others were the V-1 and V-2 rockets and the Me 262 jet fighter. But these weapons were produced too late to affect the outcome of the war.

Many other brilliant designs remained on the drawing-board, including plans for a transatlantic bomber and a vertical take-off fighter. Shortages of raw materials and Allied bombing also hindered progress.

The six-month campaign to control Guadalcanal Island

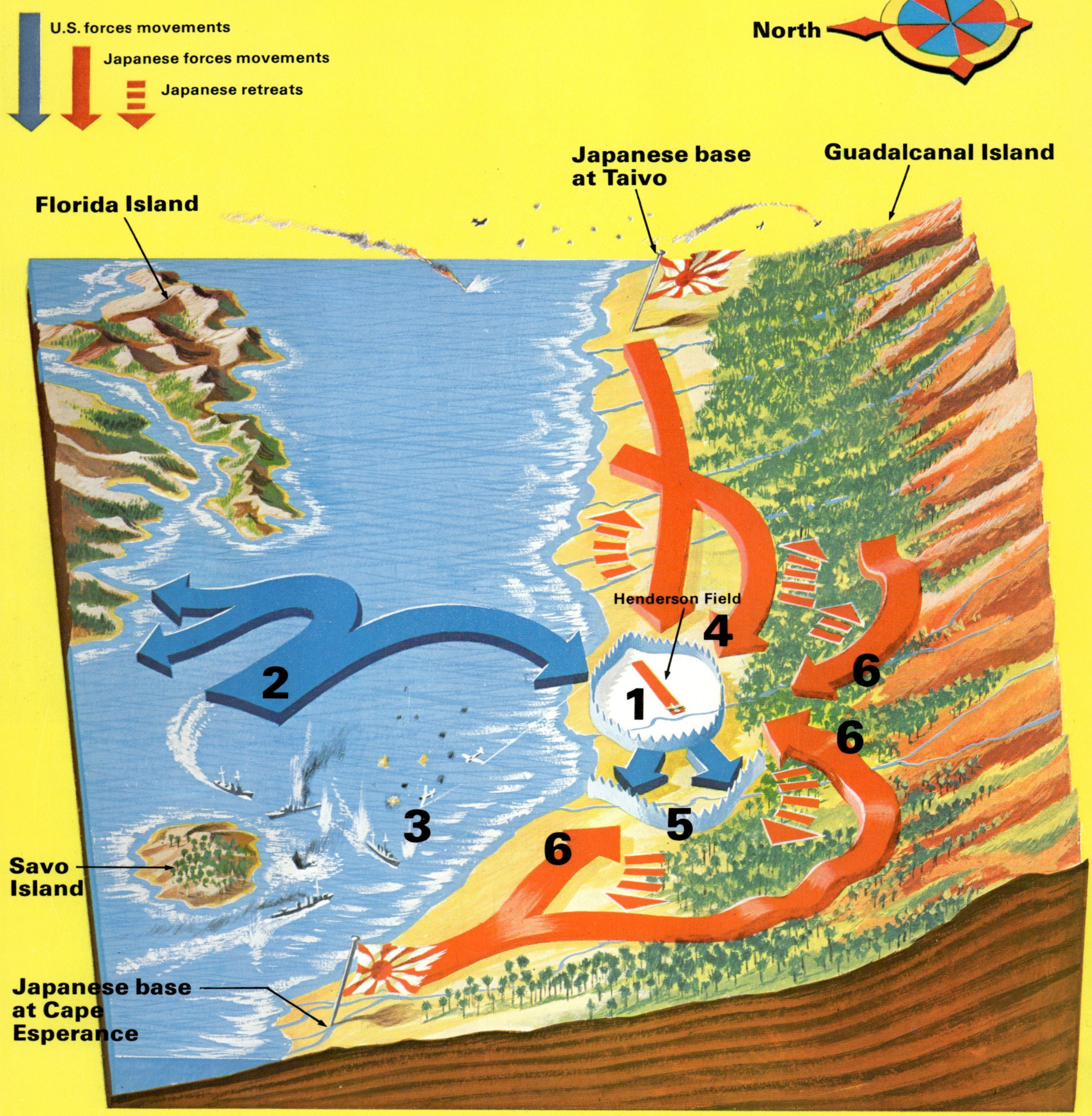

U.S. forces movements
Japanese forces movements
Japanese retreats

North

Florida Island

Japanese base at Taivo

Guadalcanal Island

Henderson Field

Savo Island

Japanese base at Cape Esperance

Guadalcanal was in the front line of the Japanese advance towards Australia. In August 1942, Japanese troops had almost completed an airfield on the island (**1**), when the Americans landed 16,000 men on it and the nearby islands (**2**).

The Japanese Navy struck back two days later and drove off the U.S. Fleet, sinking four cruisers in the first of many naval battles fought off Guadalcanal (**3**). On land, Japanese troops attacked the defence perimeter, but suffered heavy losses. Even with reinforcements they failed to break the American lines (**4**).

The Americans then pushed their defence perimeter out towards the west of the island (**5**). But now the Japanese were able to put even more men on the island, and in October and November launched heavy attacks from three directions against the Americans' perimeter round the airfield (**6**). But the line held, and the Americans began to gain the upper hand at sea and in the air, helped by a fighter base built next to the main airfield, which was called Henderson Field.

The Japanese began to evacuate the island in February 1943. They had lost 24,000 men. American losses were 2,000.

DEFEAT OF JAPAN

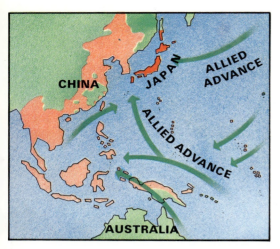

▲**Regaining the vast area** conquered by the Japanese took three years of fighting by land, sea and air.

The American victory at Midway in June 1942 was the turning point of the Pacific War. But it took another three years to defeat Japan. Hundreds of islands had to be recaptured. At first the Allies did not have the ships, planes and men needed for this.

War on the islands

After Midway the Japanese pushed on south towards Australian-held Port Moresby on New Guinea. For this offensive, and to cover the approaches to their home islands, they began to build an airfield on Guadalcanal, in the Solomon Islands.

The Americans saw that this base would threaten their supply lines. On August 7, 1942, they landed 16,000 men on Guadalcanal and seized the almost completed airfield. The Japanese counter-attacked fiercely. For six months there was continuous land, sea and air fighting for the island and its vital airfield.

The Japanese failed to dislodge the Americans. After heavy defeats they gave up the attempt. The Americans then set about taking the rest of the Solomon Islands. The task took them almost two years.

Amphibious warfare

In Europe the Allies won the war in spite of costly mistakes. In the Pacific the Americans won a new and difficult type of war and made very few mistakes. They mastered a new type of amphibious warfare. And they created many new weapons. Among them were various types of landing craft, some of which fired rockets, and the strange-looking LVT (Landing Vehicle Tracked), known as the Buffalo.

The Americans also learnt to keep their armies and naval forces in action in very difficult conditions. Special supply and repair ships stayed close to the front line. Damaged ships didn't always have to go to the United States or Hawaii for repairs.

Perhaps the most important of the U.S. forces in the Pacific were the 'Seabees'. They were the construction troops who moved in as soon as an island or beachhead was taken and built or repaired roads, wharves and airfields, as well as building barracks and hospitals.

The Americans fought a desperate and skilful enemy in terrible conditions and over a huge area. They had heavy losses in men and material. But in the end they won control of sea and air and gradually reconquered the islands that the Japanese had overrun in 1941 and 1942.

The capture of Tarawa

Several battles stand out as specially important in the Pacific War. In November 1943 the heavily fortified Tarawa Atoll was captured. American losses were heavy. But the way was opened for a central Pacific offensive.

In June 1944, in the Battle of the Philippine Sea, the Americans destroyed 400 enemy aircraft, losing only 30 themselves. The Japanese lost two carriers in the battle. In another sea and air battle in October, in Leyte Gulf, the Japanese did well at first, but later lost most of their remaining naval forces.

In Burma, on the western edge of Japan's conquests, British, Indian and Chinese forces gradually mastered the art of jungle warfare, helped by their air superiority. After defeating the Japanese at Imphal in March 1944, they pushed them back through Burma and Malaya.

In November 1944 the U.S.A.F. could begin bombarding Japan with B-29 Superfortresses based in the Marianas, which they had captured in July. The B-29 was the biggest plane to be produced in any numbers during the war.

Most of the bombs used were incendiaries (fire-bombs), which caused a huge loss of life among Japanese civilians. The Japanese withdrew fighters from the Pacific to defend the homeland. But as in Germany, the bombing didn't have much effect on production. It suffered more from the loss of raw materials when the islands and countries of South East Asia were recaptured.

Hiroshima and Nagasaki

The war against Japan ended in August 1945. A terrible new weapon, the atomic bomb, was used against two Japanese cities, Hiroshima and Nagasaki. More than 100,000 people, mostly civilians, were killed. Japan surrendered a few days later, on August 14.

The Allies had won the war before the atomic bombs were dropped. They were masters of the sea and air round Japan. Russia was about to add her weight to the Allied side. Thousands of tons of Japanese shipping were being sunk. Troops and equipment were being brought from Europe to invade the home islands. Japan could not win. Like the bombing of German and Japanese cities, the dropping of the atomic bombs is now seen by many as a terrible mistake.

Two atomic bombs of different types were built by the Americans and used by them against the Japanese cities of Hiroshima and Nagasaki. The first bomb was dropped on Hiroshima by a B-29 Superfortress, America's biggest bomber, on August 6, 1945. Seventy thousand people died instantly, and another 150,000 died later from burns and sickness caused by atomic radiation from the bomb.

◄**Hiroshima** flattened by 'Little Boy,' the first atomic bomb. The explosion's blast was hotter than the Sun itself.

TIMECHART: 1939-1945

1939
- September 1 — Germans invade Poland in 'blitzkrieg' attack.
- September 3 — Great Britain and France declare war on Germany.
- September 27 — Warsaw surrenders. Germany and Russia divide Poland.

1940
- April 9 — Germans invade Denmark and Norway.
- May 10 — Germans invade Holland, Belgium and Luxembourg.
- June 4 — British evacuate their defeated army from Dunkirk.
- June 25 — France surrenders to the Germans.
- September 15 — Battle of Britain at its climax.

1941
- February 7 — German Afrika Korps arrives in Libya to help Italians.
- April 24 — Greece surrenders to Germans after an 18-day campaign.
- June 22 — Germans invade Russia.
- September 26 — Germans win battle round Kiev. Half a million Russian soldiers killed or captured.
- December 2 — German attack on Moscow fails.
- December 7 — Japanese attack U.S. naval base at Pearl Harbour and invade Malaya and Philippines.

1942
- February 15 — Singapore surrenders to Japanese.
- May 30 — R.A.F. attack German city of Cologne with 1,000 bombers.
- June 3–7 — Americans win Battle of Midway. Turning point of Pacific War.
- August 7 — American troops land on Guadalcanal – 6-month battle begins.
- August 19 — Raid on Dieppe by British and Canadian troops.
- October 23 — Battle of El Alamein.

1943
- January 31 — German Sixth Army surrenders to Russians at Stalingrad.
- July 5 — Battle of Kursk begins.
- July 10 — Invasion of Sicily by British and Americans.
- September 7 — Italy surrenders, but Germans in Italy continue fight.
- November 20 — American attack on Tarawa opens central Pacific campaign.

1944
- June 6 — D-Day. Allied invasion of Normandy.
- June 7 — Japanese attack on Imphal fails and they retreat from the borders of India.
- June 19 — Japanese Navy heavily defeated in Battle of the Philippine Sea.
- December 16 — Battle of the Bulge. German Army's last offensive in west.

1945
- March 7 — First Allied units cross the Rhine.
- April 30 — Hitler commits suicide as Russians capture Berlin.
- May 8 — Germans surrender. End of war in Europe.
- August 6 — Atomic bomb dropped on Hiroshima. Japan surrenders 8 days later. End of World War 2.

IMPROVING AND STORING GAME PIECES

The pieces on pages 20-21 are designed to be cut out and used as they are. They will last a long time if you strengthen them with thin card as shown in the illustration below.

The best card to use is the sort that postcards are printed on. Glue the pieces onto the card, either separately or in groups, and carefully cut them out with a craft knife or scissors.

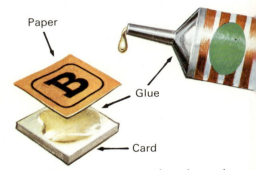

You will need to store the pieces in a safe place, otherwise some will get lost. Use an envelope or a small cardboard box for each game's pieces. Mark the name of the game on the front. Keep all four sets in a drawer or on a shelf.

Making your own pieces

When you are used to playing the games, you may wish to use more exciting and colourful pieces than the paper pieces supplied with this book.

With some practice you can make your own pieces out of card. You can cut them to the shape of the various men and machines used in the games. Enamel modelling paints are best for colouring, as they give a hard-wearing glossy finish.

A good idea is to use miniature figures on the gameboards. They can be bought from any good model shop. They are made in a lot of different sizes, so you can choose the right ones for each gameboard.

Model aircraft to 1/144 scale are ideal for Air Assault. You can mount them on bases to make them easier to handle on the board. Get a long pin or piece of wire and heat it carefully over a candle, holding it with tweezers. Poke it into the belly of the plane, at the point of balance. When it is firmly joined, attach a base of modelling clay to the bottom end of the pin. Flatten the bottom of the base, and your plane will be ready to do battle in the skies over France.

THE RULES FOR WINTER WAR

A game for two players

December, 1943, on the Eastern Front. German troops guarding a railway junction in occupied Russia have three enemies to fight—the advancing Red Army, local partisans, and the savagely cold Russian winter.

1 The pieces

	PIECE	MOVES PER TURN	ATTACK RANGE	FIGHTING VALUE (F.V.)
GERMANS	4 Pz Kw IV TANKS	UP TO 3 SPACES	4	5
	2 STUG III ASSAULT GUNS	"	3	3
	2 MOTORIZED INFANTRY UNITS	"	3	2
	2 ARTILLERY BATTERIES	"	2	8	2
	4 INFANTRY UNITS	"	2	1	1
RUSSIANS	4 T-34 TANKS	"	4	5
	5 SKI INFANTRY UNITS	"	4	1	2
	2 ARTILLERY BATTERIES	"	2	8	2
	4 INFANTRY UNITS	"	2	1	1
PARTISANS	1 PARTISAN GROUP	"	2	1	1
	4 BLANK DECOY PIECES	—	—	—

ATTACK CHART

DICE THROW	EQUAL FIGHTING VALUE	ATTACKER HAS HIGHER F.V.	ATTACKER HAS DOUBLE OR MORE F.V.
6	DEFENDER DESTROYED	DEFENDER DESTROYED	DEFENDER DESTROYED
5	DEFENDER RETREATS		
4		DEFENDER RETREATS	
3	ATTACKER RETREATS		DEFENDER RETREATS
2		ATTACKER RETREATS	
1	ATTACKER DESTROYED	ATTACKER DESTROYED	ATTACKER RETREATS

2 Extras

A dice
Two counters

3 Object of the game

One player controls the German forces, the other controls the Russian forces.

The Russian player has to capture the railway junction in the German-occupied town within **12** moves. To do this, he has to move any one of his pieces onto the orange space.

The German player wins if the Russian player cannot do this.

4 Starting the game

The German player chooses **eight** of his pieces and puts them, one to a space, within the town and its defence line. He leaves his other six pieces off the board.

The Russian player places all his pieces, one to a space, on the grey spaces at the bottom of the board.

The five partisan pieces, of which four are blank decoys, are shuffled face down and placed, one to a space, on the five spaces marked with flames.

Put one counter at **0** on the thermometer, and one counter at **12** on the timer.

The Russian player takes the first turn, moving as many or as few of his pieces as he likes. Each time that he **finishes** his turn, move the counter on the timer down a number. If it reaches **0**, the German player has won the game.

5 Freezing up

The Germans are not as well prepared as the Russians for the freezing winter cold.

To find out the temperature, the German player throws the dice at the **beginning** of each of his turns. Each pip shown represents 5° below zero (so a 3, for instance, equals −15°). Move the counter on the thermometer to the temperature indicated.

If it is **25°** or **30°** below zero, the German player **cannot move** his tanks, guns or artillery. His motorized infantry can only move a maximum of two spaces.

6 Moving

The number of spaces each piece can move is marked in section **1**.

Pieces cannot move through or onto a space occupied by an **enemy** piece (except for German pieces hunting for partisans—see section **7**), but pieces can pass through spaces occupied by pieces of their own side.

Pieces must end their moves on unoccupied spaces.

Only infantry and partisan pieces can enter high ground or forests.

Russian pieces cannot move through the defence line—but all German pieces can.

7 The partisans

A Russian partisan group is sabotaging road and rail links between the town and the outside world. The German player **must find it** before he can bring the six pieces from the side of the board into the game.

To find the group, he must move pieces onto partisan pieces, which are immediately turned face up. If they are decoys, the search goes on.

When the Germans find the real partisan piece, the Russian player decides whether it should move away or fight. The remaining blank pieces are then removed from the board. The German player can bring pieces from the side of the board into the game in his **next** turn. They enter the board through the arrowed space at the top of the board.

The partisan group joins the Russian forces and continues in play as an infantry unit.

8 Attacking

Players can make attacks at the end of each turn, after they have moved all their pieces.

Each piece can attack **once** per turn. Pieces can attack only when their fighting value (marked in section **1**) is **equal to** or **higher than** that of the piece they are attacking.

Two or more pieces can jointly attack one enemy piece, in which case their fighting values are added together.

The **attacking player** throws the dice, and the result of the attack is read off on the chart. Even if two or more pieces are making a joint attack, the dice is thrown **once** only.

Pieces which are destroyed are removed from the board. Pieces which retreat must move back two spaces, the Germans northwards and the Russians to the south. Any piece that cannot move back at least one row because its route is blocked is removed from the board.

9 Defences

Defending pieces inside the town and defence line, in forests, farms or on high ground, have their fighting values **doubled** when they are being attacked from **outside** these areas.

10 Tips to win the game

● **Russian player:** Advance as fast as you can. Your best chance of destroying German pieces is when they are in the open, looking for the partisan piece.
● **German player:** The sooner you can find the partisan piece, and start bringing reinforcements onto the board, the better. From then on it's a holding action—you only have to last out for twelve moves to win.

THE RULES FOR CARRIER

A game for two players.
Japanese and American carrier fleets struggle for control of a group of islands in the Pacific Ocean.

1 Pieces

EACH PLAYER HAS		MOVES PER TURN
SHIPS	3 AIRCRAFT CARRIERS	UP TO 4 SPACES
	2 CRUISERS	" " 3 "
AIRCRAFT	10 BOMBERS	" " 15 "
	5 FIGHTERS	" " 10 "
AMPHIBIOUS ASSAULT GROUPS	4 AMPHIBIANS	" " 2 "

STACKING

STACK OF FOUR AIRCRAFT

AIRCRAFT CARRIER OR BASE

A MAXIMUM OF FOUR AIRCRAFT CAN BE ABOARD A CARRIER OR ON A BASE AT THE SAME TIME

2 Extras
A dice
Paper and pencil

3 Object of the game
One player controls the Japanese forces. The other player controls the American forces.
The first player **either** to take both of the other player's bases by landing amphibian forces on them, **or** to destroy the three enemy carriers, wins the game.

4 Starting the game
Draw up a list of each player's ships and amphibians on the piece of paper. Record 'hits' (see section **6**) on ships by marking 'X's against them on the list.
Both players place their ship and amphibian pieces, one to a space, on any of the arrowed starting spaces on their side of the board.
Each player then places any **two** of his aircraft in each of his two bases. The remaining planes are placed on carriers, not more than four to a carrier.

There can never be more than one ship, or four of a player's aircraft, on a space.

The American player moves first. The two players then move in turn until one or other wins the game.

5 Moving
Different pieces can move different numbers of spaces (listed in section **1**) in a turn.
Each player can move all, some or none of his pieces in his turn.
The order in which pieces should be moved is:
1 Planes sent out on missions in the previous turn must return to one of their player's bases or carriers to refuel. Any plane that cannot reach a base or carrier within one move is destroyed. (This move does not apply in each player's first turn, when planes have not yet taken off.)
2 Ships move.
3 Aircraft move again, if required.
4 Attacks are made (see section **6**).

Ships must move round (not over) islands. Amphibian forces can only move onto islands when attacking bases.

6 Attacks
After moving his pieces, a player can then decide to make attacks. Each piece can attack **once** per turn. Ships firing at aircraft can fire **once** at each aircraft in range.

The order in which attacks are made is:

1 Ship vs. ship or amphibian
Only a cruiser can attack other ships. It can attack any ship or amphibian within a range of three spaces.
The attacking player throws the dice. A **5** or **6** scores a hit.

2 Ship or amphibian vs. aircraft
All ships and amphibians can attack aircraft on the same space as themselves.
The attacking player throws the dice **once** for each aircraft in range. A **6** scores a hit.

3 Aircraft vs. aircraft
Aircraft move onto the same space as enemy aircraft to make an attack.
Both players throw the dice, adding **2** if their plane is a **fighter**. If either player gets a total **2 or more** higher than the other, the loser's plane is destroyed. If not, the result is a draw and play continues.
Aircraft attacking a 'stack' of enemy planes must attack the top plane in the pile.

4 Bombers vs. ships or amphibians
The bomber moves onto the same space as the enemy vessel.
The attacking player throws the dice. A **5** or **6** scores a hit.
Bombers cannot attack ships or amphibians if an enemy plane is on the same space as the vessel—the aircraft has to be attacked first. So players can give vessels protection by keeping aircraft over them to act as 'air cover'.

One hit destroys an aircraft.
Two hits destroy a ship or amphibian.

Vessels that have been hit only once continue in play normally.
Destroyed pieces are taken off the board.

7 Capturing bases
To capture an enemy base, the attacking player must move an amphibian onto it. He holds the base only as long as his amphibian remains on it.

8 Tips on tactics
● Keep your amphibians moving steadily towards enemy bases.
● Protect 'stacks' of bombers from enemy aircraft by placing fighters on top.
● Protect aircraft carriers by keeping fighters on them.

CUT ALONG THIS DOTTED LINE ✂

CAREFULLY CUT ALONG THE DOTTED LINE. REMOVE THIS PAGE FROM THE BOOK. CUT-OUT GAME PIECES FOR **'WINTER WAR'** AND **'CARRIER'** ARE ON THE OTHER SIDE.

THE PIECES FOR WINTER WAR

PzKwIV TANKS — STUG ASSAULT GUNS — MOTORIZED INFANTRY

CUT ALL SOLID LINES

INFANTRY

ARTILLERY BATTERIES

GERMAN PIECES

T-34 TANKS — INFANTRY

ARTILLERY BATTERIES

SKI INFANTRY

BLANK DECOYS

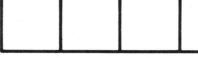

PARTISAN

RUSSIAN PIECES

THE PIECES FOR CARRIER

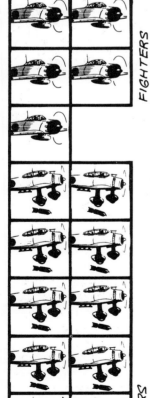
FIGHTERS

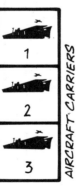
AIRCRAFT CARRIERS
1 / 2 / 3

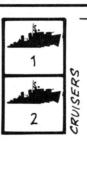
CRUISERS
1 / 2

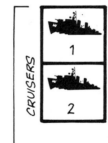
CRUISERS
1 / 2

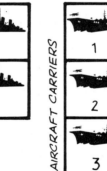
AIRCRAFT CARRIERS
1 / 2 / 3

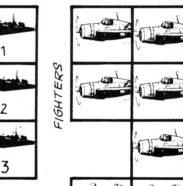
FIGHTERS

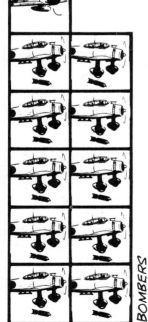
BOMBERS

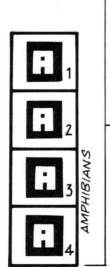
AMPHIBIANS
A 1 / A 2 / A 3 / A 4

JAPANESE FORCES

USE THIS SPINNER IF YOU DO NOT HAVE A DICE

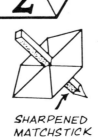

SHARPENED MATCHSTICK

AMERICAN FORCES

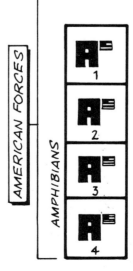
AMPHIBIANS
A 1 / A 2 / A 3 / A 4

BOMBERS

THE PIECES FOR AIR ASSAULT

B26 1 | B26 1 | B26 1

B25 1 | B25 1 | B25 1

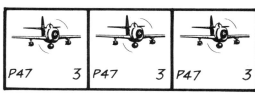
P47 3 | P47 3 | P47 3

P51 3 | P51 3 | P51 3

ALLIED AIRCRAFT

GERMAN AIRCRAFT

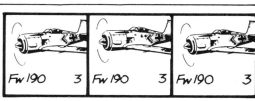
Fw190 3 | Fw190 3 | Fw190 3

BF109 2 | BF109 2 | BF109 2

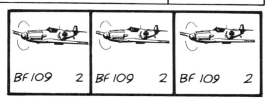
BF109 2 | BF109 2 | BF109 2

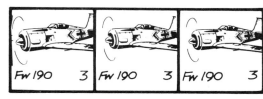
Fw190 3 | Fw190 3 | Fw190 3

THE PIECES FOR BEACH-HEAD

CRAB TANKS

BOBBIN TANKS

BULLDOZERS

FOLD DOTTED LINES

ALLIED PIECES

ALLIED INFANTRY

BRIDGE TANKS

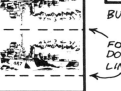
DESTROYER

GERMAN TANKS

ANTI-TANK GUNS

HEAVY ARTILLERY

GERMAN PIECES

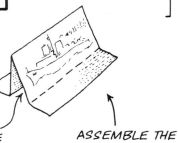
GLUE INSIDE

ASSEMBLE THE DESTROYER AND THE HEAVY ARTILLERY LIKE THIS. GLUE THE FOLDED SIDES TOGETHER TO MAKE THE PIECES STAND UPRIGHT.

INFANTRY

Carefully cut along the dotted line. Remove this page from the book. Cut-out game pieces for 'AIR ASSAULT' and 'BEACH-HEAD' are on the other side.

CUT ALONG THIS DOTTED LINE ✂

THE RULES FOR AIR ASSAULT

A game for two players

Spring 1943. An Allied bomber and fighter force crosses the Channel to attack targets in occupied France. German airfields in the area go on alert. Which side will win the fight in the sky?

1 The pieces

ALLIED AIRCRAFT	MOVES PER TURN
3 B26 MARTIN MARAUDER BOMBERS	1 SPACE
3 B25 NORTH AMERICAN MITCHELL BOMBERS	"
3 P51D NORTH AMERICAN MUSTANG FIGHTERS	UP TO 3 SPACES
3 P47 REPUBLIC THUNDERBOLT FIGHTERS	" " 3 "
GERMAN AIRCRAFT	
6 FOCKE-WULF 190 FIGHTERS	UP TO 3 SPACES
6 MESSERSCHMITT BF-109 FIGHTERS	" " 2 SPACES

2 Extras

Two packs of ordinary playing cards. Pencil and paper.

3 Object of the game

One player controls the Allied aircraft. The other player controls the Luftwaffe fighters.

Players score points by damaging and shooting down enemy planes. The Allied player also scores points by bombing target squares. The player who has the most points at the end of the game wins.

4 Setting up the board

Remove the Kings, Queens and Jacks from the two packs of playing cards (but keep the Aces–they count as 1). Each player takes a pack and shuffles it, keeping it face down. One player keeps the score with the paper and pencil.

The German player places his aircraft on the airfields (in the centre of squares outlined in white), four to each airfield.

The Allied player places his aircraft, one to a circle, in the three squares outlined in red at the top of the board.

The four coloured circles in each square show different flying heights. Blue is the lowest–5,000 feet. Yellow is 10,000 feet, orange 20,000 feet, and red 30,000 feet.

The German player starts. His planes take off from the airfields to the blue circles. This move counts as one space. They then gain height normally, moving from circle to circle.

5 Moving

Different types of plane move at different speeds. The number of spaces each plane can move in a turn is marked in section **1** and on the piece.

All planes must move at least one space each turn.

Planes can **move through** circles occupied by other planes, but must **end their move** on an unoccupied circle (unless they are attacking–see section **6**).

A move of one space can be **either** from one flying height to the next above or below it (e.g. from blue to yellow, from yellow to orange, from red to orange) **or** on the same level from one square to an adjoining square. So a fighter that can move three spaces in one turn could, for instance, climb from blue up two levels to orange in one square, and move to the orange level in an adjoining square.

> Planes cannot move diagonally between squares.

6 Attacking

A player can make attacks after he has moved all his planes. Each fighter can attack **once** each turn. Bombers cannot attack, but they can **defend** themselves.

A fighter can attack any plane in its square that is **at the same height** or **one level below it**.

Both players draw the top card from their packs. The player with the higher total of pips on his card (or cards–see below) has **damaged** the enemy plane. If his total is **double or more than double** the enemy's, the enemy plane is **shot down,** and the piece is removed from the board.

The used cards are placed on a discard pile.

Fighters **must** attack enemy planes in the same circle as themselves.

In some situations players can choose to draw a second card.
The attacker can do this if:
1 his plane is one level higher than the plane it is attacking; or
2 he is attacking a bomber; or
3 a FW 190 attacks a P-47.
The defender can do this if:
1 his plane is a B-26; or
2 his plane is a P-51 attacked by a Bf-109.

Neither player can ever draw more than two cards.

7 Damaged planes

When a plane is damaged, turn it upside down. Note what kind of a plane it is in pencil on the back of the piece, so that you can still identify it.

Damaged planes can still bomb, attack, defend, and fly at normal speed. But when attacking or defending, they **cannot** ever use a **second** card.

If a damaged plane is attacked and damaged for a second time, it is destroyed.

8 Bombing

Four targets are marked on the board. They show two railway junctions, a bridge and a factory. To bomb them, Allied B-25s or B-26s must reach them on the levels marked with **bombs** on the board.

To bomb the target, the Allied player draws the top card of his pack. If it is **red**, he scores the points allowed for a **hit**. These are marked on the circles. If it is **black**, he can draw a second card. If that is also black the bomber has missed, and **no points** are scored.

9 Anti-aircraft guns

Three anti-aircraft guns are marked on the board. The German player can fire at any Allied plane in the circles marked with explosions.

To shoot down an Allied plane at 5,000 or 10,000 feet (blue or yellow circles), the German player must draw a **6, 7, 8, 9** or **10** from the top of his pack. To shoot down a plane at 20,000 feet (orange circle), he must draw a **9** or **10**.

Anti-aircraft guns can fire **one** shot at **each** plane in range each turn.

10 Scoring

DAMAGING AN ENEMY AIRCRAFT	2 POINTS
DESTROYING AN AIRCRAFT THAT IS ALREADY DAMAGED	3 POINTS
DESTROYING AN UNDAMAGED AIRCRAFT	5 POINTS
BOMBING TARGETS	THE NUMBER OF POINTS MARKED ON THE TARGET

> There is a bonus of 15 points for either player if he destroys all enemy aircraft.

11 The end of the game

The game ends when **both players** have used up all their cards.

12 Tips on tactics

● Remember that your cards are your ammunition (for fighters, bombers, anti-aircraft guns and bombs). **Don't waste them.** The first person to run out of cards can do nothing to protect his planes, and they will be shot down like flies.

THE RULES FOR BEACH-HEAD

A game for two players

June 6, 1944 – D-Day. Allied landing forces are fighting to win a foothold in occupied France. With them come the 'funnies' – tanks adapted to beat the beach defences and to drive a wedge into the flank of Hitler's Europe.

1 The pieces

ALLIES	5 CRAB TANKS	UP TO 6 SQUARES	
	4 BOBBIN TANKS	" " 6 "	
	4 BULLDOZERS	" " 6 "	
	3 BRIDGE TANKS	" " 6 "	
	10 INFANTRY UNITS	" " 3 "	MOVES PER TURN
	1 ROYAL NAVY DESTROYER	DOES NOT MOVE	
GERMANS	6 TANKS	UP TO 6 SQUARES	
	2 ANTI-TANK GUNS	DO NOT MOVE	
	10 INFANTRY UNITS	UP TO 3 SQUARES	
	1 HEAVY ARTILLERY UNIT	DOES NOT MOVE	

2 Extras

A dice
A counter
About 20 blank squares of card, ⅝ in. x ⅝ in., to be placed on cleared obstacles.

3 Object of the game

One player controls the Allied forces, the other controls the German forces.

The Allied player wins if he gets at least two tanks (bulldozers count as tanks) and two infantry units to the southernmost row of squares on the board within 12 turns.

The German player wins if the Allied player fails to do this.

4 Starting the game

1 Put the counter on 12 on the timer.
2 The German player places his heavy artillery unit, his two anti-tank guns, and any two other pieces of his choice on the board.

The artillery unit goes in the square marked for it. The anti-tank guns go in any two of the three anti-tank gun emplacements. The other two pieces go on the arrowed squares at the bottom of the board.
3 The Allied player places the destroyer on the square marked for it, and puts any five of his other pieces anywhere on the top row of squares. Allied pieces cannot move or fire during the turn in which they enter the board.

At the end of the Allied player's turn, the counter is moved down to 11 on the timer.
4 In his next and following turns, the German player can move the two pieces in the German start squares, fire at any Allied pieces within range, and bring two more pieces onto the start squares.

Unlike Allied pieces, German pieces can fire in the turn in which they enter the board.
5 In his next and following turns, the Allied player can move pieces already on the board, fire at any German pieces within range, and bring five more pieces onto the board on the top row of squares. At the end of each turn, he moves the counter down a number on the timer.

5 Moving

The number of squares that each piece can move is listed in section **1**.

Pieces can move through squares occupied by their own side's pieces, but **not** through those occupied by enemy pieces.

All pieces must **end** their move on unoccupied squares.

Diagonal moves are not allowed.

6 Obstacles

Players must move their pieces carefully through the various obstacles marked on the board.

Forest: No piece can pass through this.
The river: Can be crossed by a bridge or over a bridge tank. Infantry can pass through the marsh square.
Minefields: Any piece can enter a minefield, but for each 'mined' square it moves onto, a dice must be thrown. A throw of 1, 2 or 3 means the piece is destroyed. 'Mined' squares can be cleared (see section **7**) by Crab tanks.

These three obstacles affect tanks and infantry alike. The remaining obstacles only affect tanks; infantry can pass through them, but tanks cannot pass them till they have been cleared.

Anti-tank obstacles must be cleared by bulldozers.
Soft sand and marsh squares must be cleared by Bobbin tanks.
Ditches can be cleared by Bobbin tanks or bridged by bridge tanks.

The **wall** can be cleared by bulldozers. The Allied player can also fire at a wall square with his destroyer – a hit clears the square. Bridge tanks can also be used to cross the wall.

7 Clearing obstacles

To clear a square, the tank piece named in the list above must end a move on it and remain in place until the beginning of the Allied player's next turn. From then on the square is cleared, and any piece of either side can move through it.

> Put a blank square over the obstacle to show that it has been cleared.

Crab tanks and bulldozers can be used any number of times, but Bobbin tanks can only clear one square each.

Bridge tanks do **not** clear obstacles. They have to stay on a river, ditch or wall square for other pieces to pass over them.

8 Firing

Players can make their pieces fire at the end of their turns, after their pieces have been moved. Each piece can fire once per turn.

The only Allied tank that can fire is the Crab. The other 'funnies' cannot make attacks.

To fire at an enemy piece:
1 Choose the piece you want to fire with, and the target you are aiming at.
2 Count the number of squares between them along vertical and horizontal (**not** diagonal) rows.
3 Throw the dice.
4 Read off the result of the attack on the chart.

A blank means you have missed. The figures show the lowest number you have to throw for the shot to hit. If, for instance, one of your tanks is attacking an infantry unit at a range of two squares, you would have to throw a **2**, **3** or **4** to make it retreat, and a **5** or **6** to destroy it.

The wall, the destroyer, and any pieces in gun emplacements or on squares directly (i.e. one row) behind the wall, count as 'concrete' targets.

Pieces that are destroyed are removed from the board.

Pieces that have to retreat must move one square straight back, the Allies to the north, the Germans to the south. If an obstacle prevents them from doing this, or if the square behind them is occupied, they are destroyed.

SELECT RANGE OF TARGET IN THE RANGE ROW · SELECT THE TARGET TYPE IN THE TARGET ROW · READ OFF RESULT IN THE SQUARES BELOW

KEY TO CHART
R = RETREAT   I = INFANTRY
D = DESTROYED   T = TANK
         C = CONCRETE

	RANGE IN SQUARES →	1			2			3			4			5			6			MORE THAN 6		
	TARGET TYPE →	I	T	C	I	T	C	I	T	C	I	T	C	I	T	C	I	T	C	I	T	C
ATTACKING TYPE	INFANTRY R	3	2		4	5		5	6		6											
	D	5	5	3	6	6																	
	TANK OR ANTI-TANK R	3	2		2	3		3	4		4	5		5	5		6						
	D	6	4		5	5		6	6	5	6	5		6	6		6	6					
	HEAVY ARTILLERY R	2	1		3	2		4	3		4	3		4	3		5	4					
	D	3	2		4	3		5	4		6	5		6	5		6	6		6	6	6	

SUPPLYING THE FRONT LINE

A Junkers 52 tri-motor transport plane ferries supplies to the Eastern Front deep in Russia. The German Army used planes and trains over long distances. Horses and lorries did the rest.

The campaigns of World War 2 involved millions of people. Most of those worked behind the front line, supplying and serving the men who did the fighting.

Supply lines were vital in all military campaigns, and many battles depended on them. The men needed food and ammunition. Their vehicles needed petrol and oil.

The Germans used rail transport a great deal. They generally fought in countries with good railways, connecting with their own excellent railway system.

Attacking the railways

The Allies paid special attention to attacking the railways in France, most of all before D-Day, to prevent German troop and supply movements. Russian partisans made continual attacks on the railways behind the Eastern Front. This meant that thousands of German soldiers had to stay guarding the lines.

From railhead to front line, lorry or horse transport was used. Horses were very important to the German Army and every regiment had its veterinary company to look after them.

Lorries were used in great numbers by all armies. They had to be supplied with fuel and kept in good repair by the transport and workshop companies. The Russians relied a great deal on lorries provided by the U.S.A. and Britain.

In an offensive supplies had to keep up with the front-line troops or the attack would fail. Military police were responsible for keeping the convoys moving. They used motor-cycles and jeeps. Engineer companies cleared blocked or mined roads and bridged rivers.

The wounded had to be looked after and brought back from the front. There had to be ambulances to take them to field hospitals. During a big offensive it was important that the wounded coming back from the front didn't slow down men and supplies going forward.

Air-lift in the east

Air supply was used by the Allies in Burma and New Guinea. In the main they used two robust transport planes for supply and casualties, the Douglas Dakota and the C-46 Curtiss Commando. The Germans relied on the three-engined Junkers 52.

Both sides used small aircraft as 'taxis' for their generals and for many tasks behind the lines. The Germans had the Fieseler Storch, the Allies the Norseman and the Lysander.

The Allies had their biggest supply problem when they invaded Normandy. They knew that they had no hope of capturing a big port at the very beginning of the campaign. So they took their own port with them. This was 'Mulberry', an artificial harbour, towed across the Channel in sections and moored off the Normandy beaches.

A month after D-Day the Allies captured the port of Cherbourg, though it had been damaged by the Germans. Even then it was impossible to keep the Allied advance continuously supplied. The offensive had to be halted on the borders of Germany. The war was prolonged.

Women at war

World War 2 was fought on such a massive scale that everyone was involved. It was the first war in which women played a major part. Women drove ambulances, ferried aircraft, worked on vital installations. They also worked in the offices in which the fighting was planned and controlled – the invisible key to efficiency in such vast military operations.

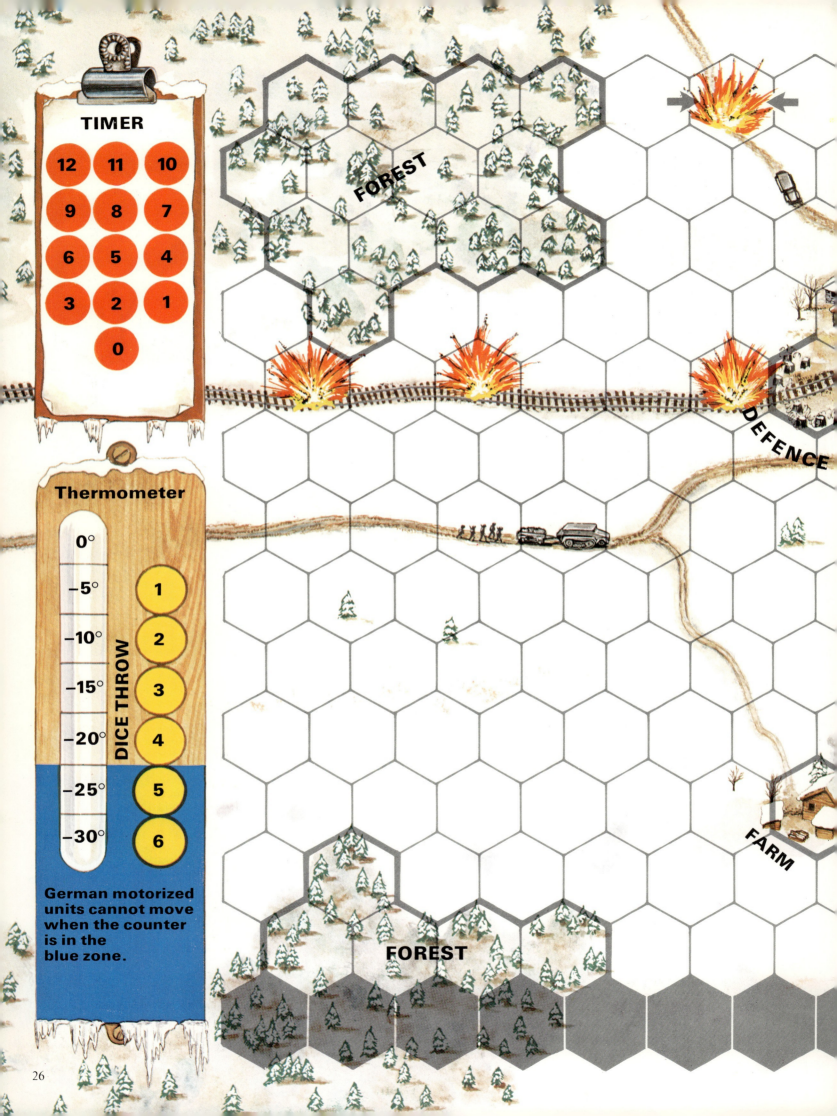

WINTER WAR

'FLAT-TOPS' IN THE PACIFIC

The two important types of ship in World War 2 were the submarine and the aircraft-carrier. The submarine was again the German's chief strength, as it had been in World War 1. The carrier won the Pacific war for the Americans.

Japan's mistake

The Japanese made a big mistake after Pearl Harbour in not attacking the only two U.S. carriers in the Pacific. These, *Enterprise* and *Lexington*, were alone, away from Hawaii, open to attack. If they had sunk them, the Japanese could have established naval supremacy in the Pacific instead of losing it within six months.

Aircraft-carriers are of two main types, fleet carriers and escort carriers. A fleet carrier carries about 100 planes and attacks the enemy fleet. An escort carrier is smaller and defends a fleet or convoy.

Carrier planes

A carrier is only as good as the planes it carries. The Americans and Japanese both had very good carrier-borne planes. British planes were never as good. This was because the U.S. and Japanese Navies had much more control over design than the Royal Navy. The best American carrier planes were the Grumman Hellcat, a fighter, and the Avenger, a torpedo-bomber, and the older Douglas Dauntless, a dive-bomber.

Each of these three types of plane had its own job to do. But they could also double as scouts, or submarine-killers. Early in the war the British still used biplanes like the Albacore and Swordfish (torpedo-bombers) on their carriers. These were later replaced by Barracudas, Fulmars, Sea Hurricanes and the sea-going version of the famous Spitfire – the Seafire.

Aircraft on lifts

Planes were carried either on deck, or in hangars below. To reach the hangars and workshops a lift or elevator was used. This could be in the middle of the deck or at the edge. To fit the elevator planes had folding wings, and sometimes forward-sloping tailplanes. The central elevator was a prime target for bombers.

An aircraft could be launched either by take-off from the flight-deck or by

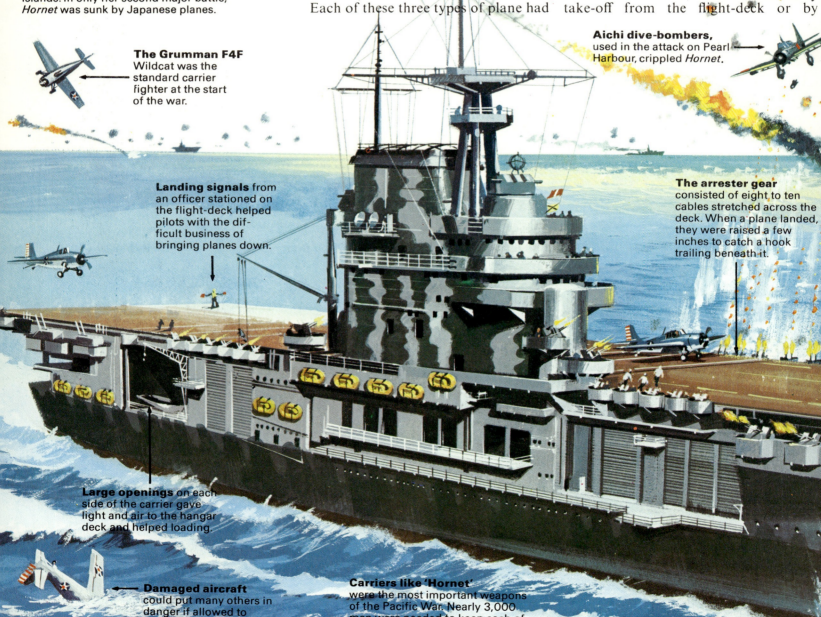

▼**This picture** shows the U.S. carrier *Hornet* during the Battle of the Santa Cruz Islands. In only her second major battle, *Hornet* was sunk by Japanese planes.

The Grumman F4F Wildcat was the standard carrier fighter at the start of the war.

Landing signals from an officer stationed on the flight-deck helped pilots with the difficult business of bringing planes down.

Large openings on each side of the carrier gave light and air to the hangar deck and helped loading.

Damaged aircraft could put many others in danger if allowed to block the deck. To prevent this, handling crews often pushed them over the side.

Aichi dive-bombers, used in the attack on Pearl Harbour, crippled *Hornet*.

The arrester gear consisted of eight to ten cables stretched across the deck. When a plane landed, they were raised a few inches to catch a hook trailing beneath it.

Carriers like 'Hornet' were the most important weapons of the Pacific War. Nearly 3,000 men were needed to keep each of them in action. Fast fleet carriers could reach speeds of up to 33 knots, were highly manoeuvrable, and could carry 100 planes.

'Hornet' was eventually sunk by a combination of dive-bomber and torpedo attacks, including a suicide attack by the Japanese squadron commander.

catapult. For a plane to take off from the deck, the carrier had to be turned into the wind. This could be inconvenient and slow down the fleet. In rough seas take-off was difficult. Catapults could be used in any conditions, even at night, and sometimes the plane could be launched direct from the hangar deck.

Dangerous landings

It was very difficult to land a plane safely on the carrier. The aircraft had a landing hook that caught on to arrester wires on the deck. Speed and height had to be judged exactly. Accidents were frequent, especially during battles, when planes might be damaged or short of fuel and pilots might be injured. Planes could overshoot and fall into the sea, or swing round and crash into parked aircraft.

A carrier's fighters could not always defend her from enemy bombers. They also had to protect their own bombers in their attacks. So the carrier had to have her own anti-aircraft guns.

One type of attack was almost impossible to avoid. This was the Japanese 'kamikaze' suicide attack. Planes, usually of obsolete types, were packed with explosives and crashed by their pilots on the decks of enemy ships. Large numbers of American ships were badly damaged in this way, including 12 carriers.

Raid on Taranto

In November 1940, 13 months before Pearl Harbour, the power of the 'flat-top' was shown for the first time, by the British, in a devastating raid on the Italian fleet at Taranto. Twenty Swordfish biplanes from the carrier *Illustrious*, 180 miles offshore, severely damaged three battleships and two cruisers. The Italians had to withdraw their main fleet to Naples.

After that, at Pearl Harbour, in the Battles of the Coral Sea, Midway and the Philippine Sea, and the assaults on Japan's fortress of islands, flat-tops and their planes played a major part.

A Hellcat pilot's lucky escape

▲ **Landing on a carrier** was always tricky. Here a U.S. Navy Hellcat fighter makes a mess of it. As the wheel goes over the edge of the flight-deck, the anti-aircraft gunners try to take cover. They've seen this sort of thing happen before.

▲ **Not even a Hellcat** can stand a landing like this, and the plane breaks in two. The auxiliary petrol tank goes flying.

▲ **The pilot** (arrowed) swims for it. He's one of the lucky ones. In a matter of minutes he'll be back on the carrier, ready to fly again.

Landing signals

 All OK
 You are too slow
 You are too fast
 You are too low
 Go round again
 Move over this way

Three lifts carried aircraft to and from the hangar deck, where planes were fuelled and armed.

Anti-aircraft guns were essential defences. *Hornet* had twenty-three 20mm guns, 16 pom-poms and 8 heavier 5-inch guns. Her gunners shot down at least 20 of her attackers in her final battle.

Wooden flight-decks were a weak point in U.S. carriers. Bombs could drop through to the hangar deck.

Grumman Avengers replaced the Dauntless as the standard torpedo-bomber.

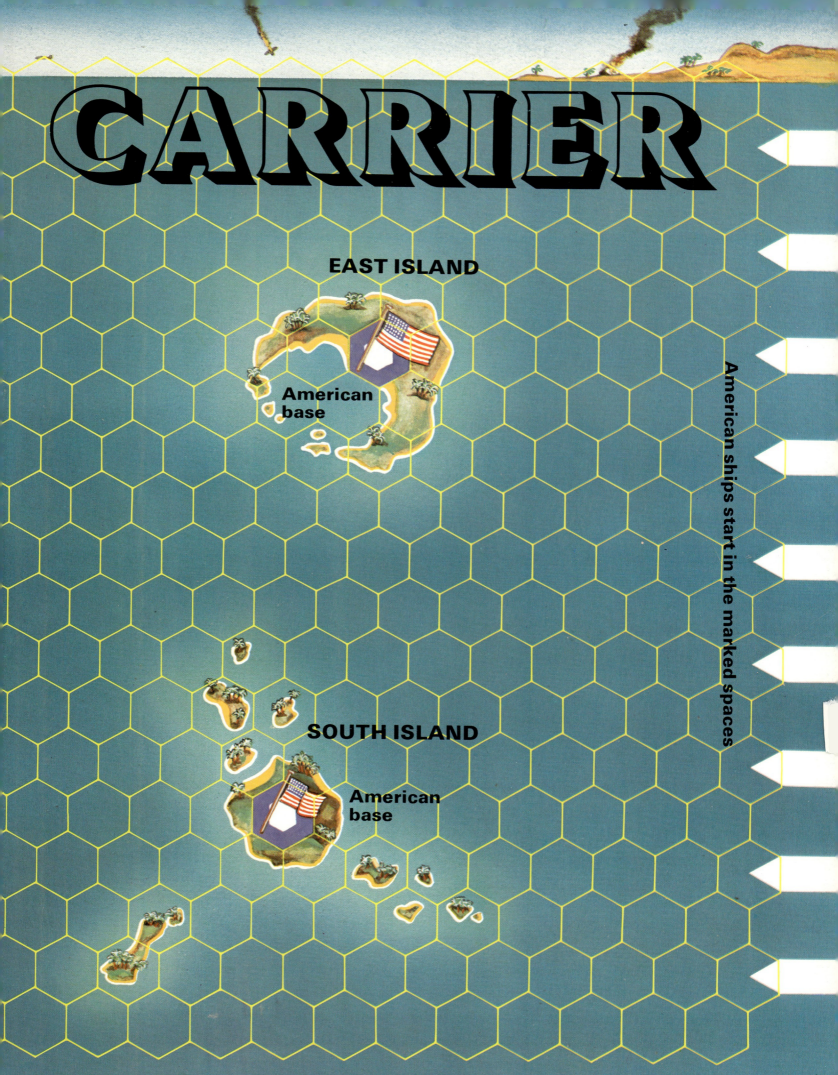

AIR WAR OVER EUROPE

In the first half of 1944, R.A.F. and U.S.A.F. heavy bombers continually raided industrial targets far inside Germany. At the same time, medium bombers dropped bombs night after night, on targets nearer home in the Low Countries and northern France. To do so, they had to avoid searchlights and anti-aircraft fire. Lots of planes were shot down.

Preparing for D-Day

Many of these raids were in preparation for the Allied invasion of Europe. From February until D-Day in June 1944, B-26 Marauders of the U.S. 9th Air Force and Mitchells, Bostons and Mosquitoes of the R.A.F. bombed railways, airfields and bridges in France by day and night. The aim of these intensive raids was to stop the Germans bringing up effective reinforcements when the invasion took place.

Many of the targets attacked by the bombers were in the middle of friendly civilian populations in occupied France. It was important that the bombing was accurate so that civilians were not hurt.

To mislead the German high command and to avoid giving any clue as to where the planned invasion was to take place, roads and railway lines to the Pas de Calais were bombed too.

It was not always easy to see how successful the bombing was. This was because aerial photographs taken afterwards did not always show whether a target had been fully destroyed.

Germany's secret weapon

The bombers also attacked the bases and storage depots of the new German secret weapon, the V-1 rockets. The experimental base at Peenemunde was also bombed, but development was not stopped. The Germans were able to start firing the weapon in June 1944. Firing only stopped when the launching sites were overrun by ground forces.

When the Allied invasion took place on June 6, its success proved how effective the bombing policy had been. German transport was so disrupted that sufficient forces could not be brought up to stop the invaders.

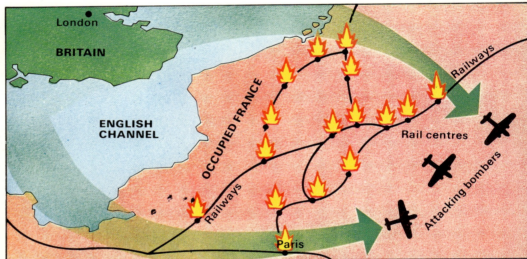

The yellow stripe on the tail shows the plane belonged to the 386th Bombardment Group of the U.S. 9th Air Force's 99th Bombardment Wing.

The fuselage was 58 feet long.

The letter next to the American star was used to identify individual planes.

The tail gunner was the most strongly armed. He had twin machine-guns, each with 1,500 rounds.

The letters RU denoted the plane's squadron – the 554th.

▼**German flak defences** took a heavy toll of Allied bombers (**A**). Outlying batteries (**B**) first tried to disrupt their formations. Closer in, several batteries concentrated fire into a 'box' (**C**) through which the bombers had to pass in order to reach the target area (**D**).

▲**Medium bombers,** fighter-bombers and fighters armed with rockets attacked roads and railways in northern France and the Low Countries. Heavy bombers made the long run into Germany. Their targets included the V-1 rocket launching sites, airfields and submarine bases.

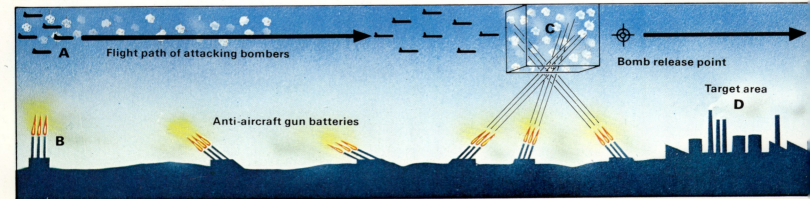

Backbone of the U.S. 9th Air Force

The Martin B-26 Marauder suffered such appalling losses when it was first brought into service with the U.S. Air Force that it was nicknamed 'The Widow Maker.'

Yet when the early teething troubles had been overcome and its performance had improved, the bomber became an excellent combat aircraft. It could take so much punishment and still go on flying that its overall losses amounted to only one plane in every sortie.

Its design was ideal for a medium-weight bomber. It was fast and simply built. This made it an easy aeroplane to mass-produce.

The B-26 carried enough fuel for a cruising range of 1,150 miles. Its maximum speed was 282 m.p.h. It was armed with four fuselage-mounted cannon and up to seven machine-guns, and it could drop 5,200 pounds of bombs.

Two powerful Pratt & Whitney engines drove the four-bladed Curtiss propellers.

The wing span was 71 feet.

The crew consisted of a pilot, co-pilot, navigator, radio operator, dorsal gunner, tail gunner and, sometimes, a waist gunner.

The nose held the bomb sight and two machine-guns.

Two cannon for strafing targets were mounted on each side of the fuselage.

The bomb load was usually sixteen 250lb bombs.

Rivals in the sky

North American B-25 Mitchell bomber
Range: 1,350 miles.
Speed: 315 m.p.h.
Ten machine-guns, 3,000lb bomb load.

Republic P-47 Thunderbolt fighter
Range: 637 miles.
Speed: 433 m.p.h.
Eight machine-guns.

North American P-51 Mustang escort fighter
Range: 1,300 miles.
Speed: 437 m.p.h. (with a Rolls Royce Merlin engine).
Six machine-guns.

Focke-Wulf FW-190 fighter
Range: 592 miles.
Speed: 416 m.p.h.
Two machine-guns and four cannon.

Messerschmitt Bf-109 fighter
Speed: 357 m.p.h.
Two machine-guns and two cannon in each wing.

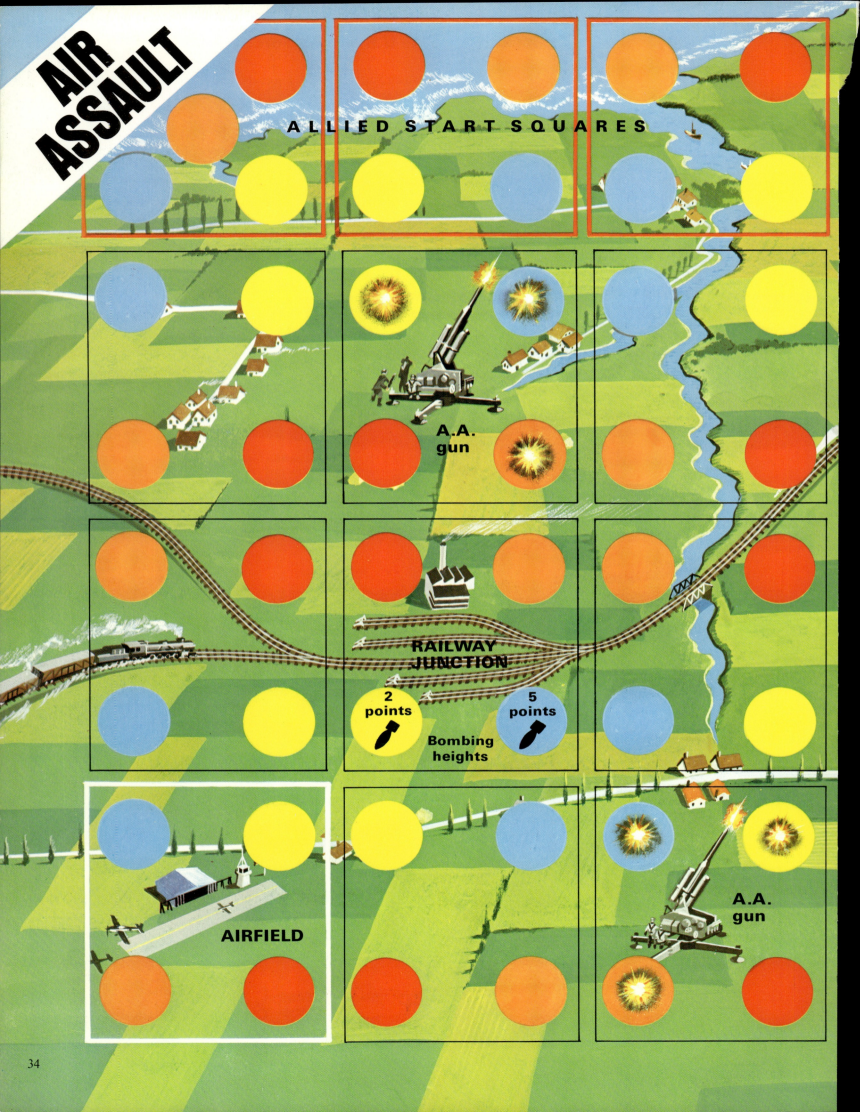

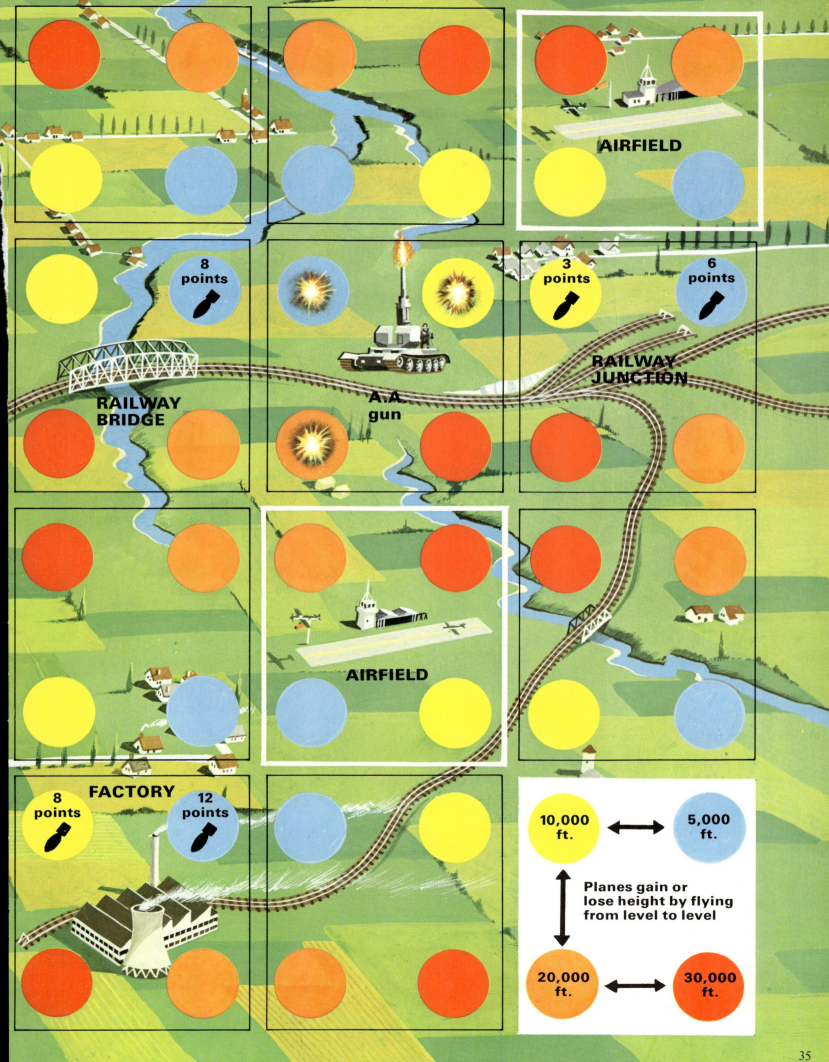

▲ **Crawling up beaches** at only 1½ m.p.h., Sherman 'Crab' tanks swept a ten-foot path through minefields with flails. The weighted ends exploded mines in the tank's path.

CLEARING THE BEACHES

The British and Canadian raid on Dieppe in 1942 taught the Allies a lot about the problems they would face in invading France.

In June 1944, the German defences were still incomplete. But there was a strong line of coastal artillery, beach-works and mines along the French coast. The Allies had to break through these in large enough numbers to hold off any German counter-attack. The weapons that helped them to do this were the 'Funnies'.

Tanks with two tasks

These were specially adapted tanks. Each had a special job to do on D-Day. But most of them could work as ordinary tanks too, to support the infantry. Where they were used the infantry was able to advance. The Americans decided to do without them on Omaha Beach. There the infantry's task was so difficult that the invasion almost failed.

First to land on D-Day were the D.D. tanks. (D.D. stands for Duplex Drive, a code name.) These were Sherman tanks adapted for swimming. They could swim to shore from as far as 3,000 yards out, presenting a small target. The Germans had never seen them before and thought they were just boats.

Tracked mine-sweepers

On the beach the tanks could use their guns to support the infantry in the normal way. But because of mines they had to wait to advance until the next Funny, the Crab, had done its job.

Crabs (also called Flails) were Sherman tanks fitted with chains. These beat the ground and exploded any mines in the way so long as they were not buried too deeply.

Most beaches ended in a steep sea-wall. To cross it, a prefabricated bridge was brought on a tank. When the bridge was in place, the D.D. tank could move through the path cleared by the Crabs, over the bridge and the sea-wall. It could then attack the enemy defences.

Bridges, and fascines to fill in anti-tank ditches, were usually carried by an adapted Churchill tank, the A.V.R.E. (Armoured Vehicle Royal Engineers).

On soft sand the Bobbin was needed. This was an A.V.R.E. that laid down a canvas carpet so that wheeled vehicles could cross the sand.

Armoured bulldozers

Armoured bulldozers moved around the beach clearing obstacles. Engineers still had to go on foot, exposed to fire, to plant demolition charges. But the Funnies made the task easier and less dangerous. They looked funny but they worked.

The Germans improvised and invented special weapons too. They built armoured vehicles on tank chassis they had available. Their tank recovery crews had done an efficient job in Russia and North

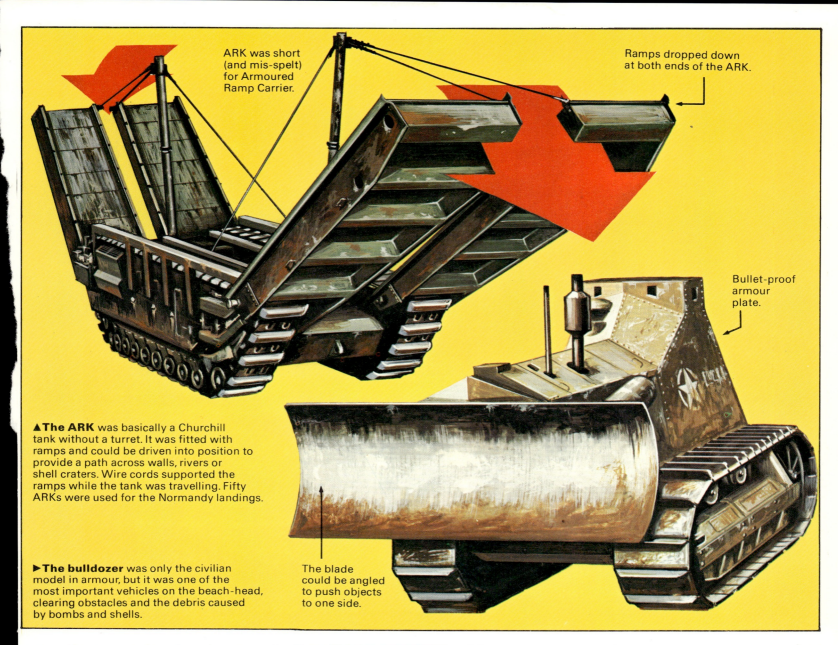

ARK was short (and mis-spelt) for Armoured Ramp Carrier.

Ramps dropped down at both ends of the ARK.

Bullet-proof armour plate.

▲ **The ARK** was basically a Churchill tank without a turret. It was fitted with ramps and could be driven into position to provide a path across walls, rivers or shell craters. Wire cords supported the ramps while the tank was travelling. Fifty ARKs were used for the Normandy landings.

▶ **The bulldozer** was only the civilian model in armour, but it was one of the most important vehicles on the beach-head, clearing obstacles and the debris caused by bombs and shells.

The blade could be angled to push objects to one side.

Africa. With specially adapted tanks and other vehicles fitted with winches and cranes, they would sometimes dash in and drag away a disabled tank even before the battle was over.

Motorized artillery

The Germans needed a lot of mobile artillery for their war against Russia. Obsolete PzKw II chassis were used to power the Wespe, a useful 105 mm howitzer. Czech chassis were used for the Hetzer tank-destroyer and Marder mobile gun. Obsolete PzKw III chassis carried a widely used infantry support gun, the Sturmgeschutz.

The Russians too were good at inventing strange weapons. The Katyusha was just a series of crude rocket tubes mounted on a lorry. But it was a terrifying support weapon. The Germans later tried the same thing, mounting a Nebelwerfer rocket battery on a Maultier half-tracked lorry.

▶ **The Bobbin tank** laid a canvas mat on soft sand where wheeled vehicles would otherwise have got bogged down. The mats were generally about 100 yards long.

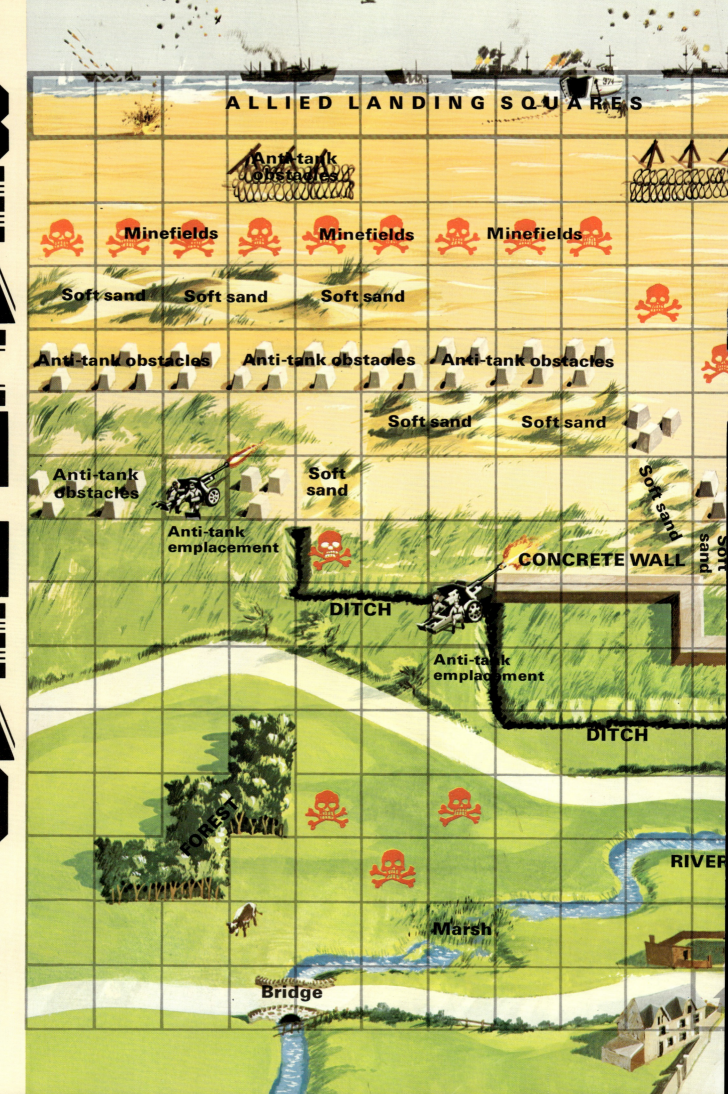

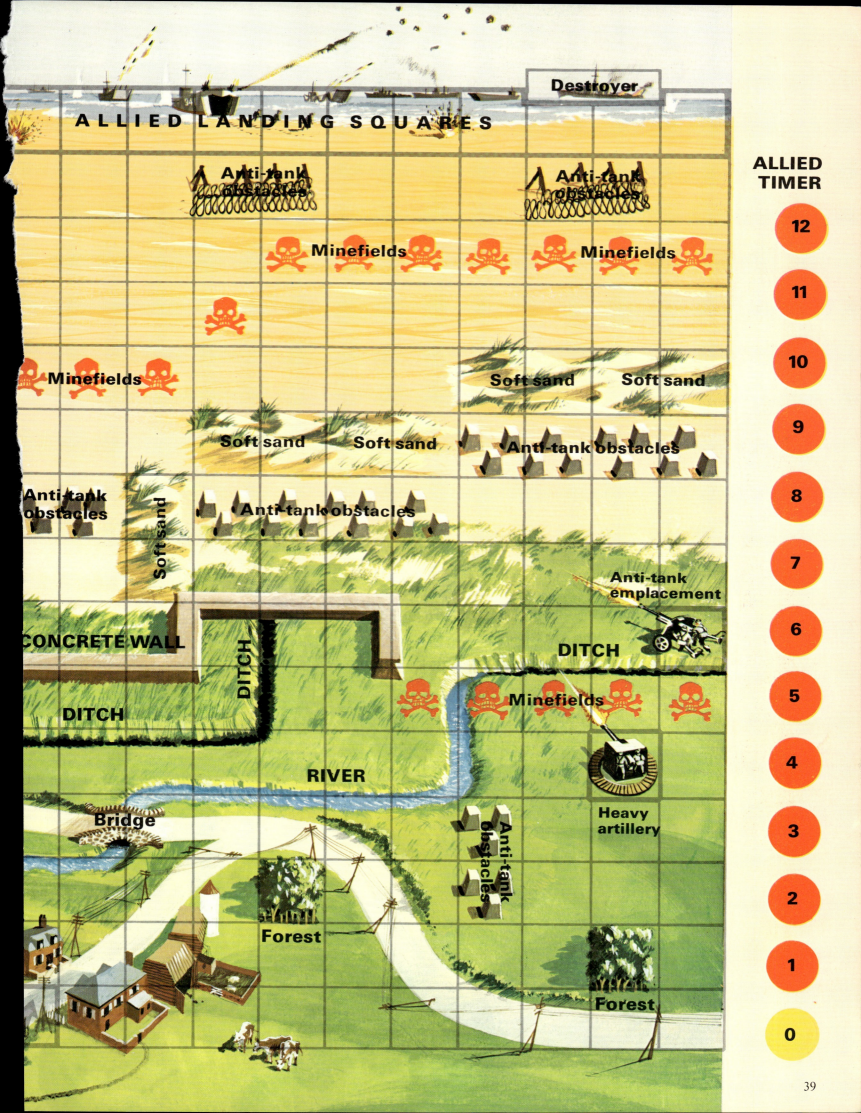

INDEX

acoustic torpedo, 11
Africa korps, 12, 16
Aichi D3A dive-bomber, 8, 28
aircraft-carriers, 8, 28
Albacore biplane, 28
amphibious warfare, 15
anti-aircraft guns, 11, 29
Ardennes, 13
ARK, the (Armoured Ramp Carrier), 37
armoured bulldozers, 36, 37
Atlantic, Battle of, 10-11
atomic bomb, 15
Australia, 14
Austria, 4
Axis advance, 4

B-29 Superfortress bombers, 15
Barracuda, 28
Battle of Britain, 4, 16
Belgium, invasion of, 4, 16
Beretta pistol, 2
Berlin, 7, 13, 16
Bismarck, 10
blitzkrieg, 4, 5, 6
Bobbin tank, 36, 37
Boston bombers, 32
Bren-gun, 2
Browning heavy machine-gun, 9
Buffalo landing craft, 15
Bulge, Battle of the, 13, 16
Burma, 15
    air supply in, 25

C-46 Curtiss Commando, 25
Caen, 13
Churchill tank, 36, 37
conning-tower, 11
Coral Sea, Battle of the, 8, 29
Crete, paratroop invasion of, 4
Czechoslovakia, 4

D-Day, 12, 13, 16, 25, 32, 36
D.D. tanks, 36
Denmark, invasion of, 4, 16
depth charges, 11
Dieppe, raid on, 16, 36
Dornier, 10
Douglas Dakota, 25
Douglas Dauntless, 8, 28
Douglas Devastator, 8
Dunkirk, 4, 16

Eastern Front, 25
El Alamein, Battle of, 12, 16
Enterprise, 28
escort system, 11

Fieseler Storch, 25
Focke-Wulf Condor bomber, 10
Focke-Wulf FW-190 fighter, 7, 33
Fulmar, 28
Funnies (adapted tanks), 36

German Navy, 10
G.M.C. trucks, 6
Graf Spee, 10
Greece, invasion of, 4, 16

Grumman Avenger, 28, 29
Grumman, Hellcat, 28, 29
Grumman Wildcat, 28
Guadalcanal Island, 14, 15, 16
guns, tank, 7
Gurkhas, 9

Hawaii, 8
Hedgehog, the, 11
Heinkel, 10
Henschel Hs 129, 7
Hetzer tank-destroyer, 37
Hiroshima, 15, 16
Hitler, 4, 12, 13, 16
Holland, invasion of, 4, 16
Hong Kong, 8
Hood, 10
Hornet, 28, 29
howitzer, 37

Illustrious, 29
Ilyushin, Il 2, 7
Indian Army, 9
Italy, occupation of, 12, 16

Japanese forces, 8, 14, 15
jeeps, 25
jungle warfare, 9, 15
Junkers 52, 25

kamikaze attack, 29
Katyusha, 37
Kesselring, 12
Kursk, Battle of, 7, 12, 16
KV-1 tanks, 6, 7

landing signals, 28, 29
Leningrad, siege of, 6
Lexington, 28
Leyte Gulf, Battle of, 15
Luftwaffe, 4, 10
Luxembourg, invasion of, 16
LVT landing craft, 15
Lysander, 25

Malaya, invasion of, 8, 15, 16
Marder mobile gun, 37
Martin B-26 Marauders, 32, 33
Me 262 jet fighter, 13
Messerschmitt Bf-109, 7, 33
Messerschmitt 163A rocket fighter, 13
Midway, Battle of, 8, 15, 16, 29
military police, 25
Mitchell B25 bombers, 32, 33
Mitsubishi Zero fighter, 8
Mosquitoes, 32
Mulberry (artificial harbour), 25
Mustang P-51 escort fighter, 33

Nagasaki, 15
Nakajima B5N torpedo-bomber, 8
Nazi Party, 4
New Guinea, 8, 15
    air supply in, 25
Normandy, invasion of, 13, 25, 37
Norseman, 25

North Africa campaign, 12
Norway, invasion of, 4, 16

Odessa, 6
Omaha Beach, 36

Pacific Fleet, 8
Pacific War, 8, 15, 16, 28
Panther, 7
Panzer Division, 6
Panzerkampfwagen, 6
Pearl Harbour, 8, 16, 28, 29
Peenemunde, 32
Philippines, 8
Philippine Sea, Battle of the, 15, 16, 29
Poland, invasion of, 4, 6, 16
PzKw II tanks, 4, 37
PzKw III tanks, 6, 37
PzKw IV tanks, 6, 7
PzKw V tanks, 7
PzKw VI tanks, 7

Reichstag, 13
Republic P-47 Thunderbolt fighter, 33
Rommel, 12
Russia, invasion of, 4, 6, 16

St. Lô, 13
Santa Cruz Islands, Battle of the, 28
Seabees, 15
Seafire, 28
Sea Hurricane, 28
Sherman 'Crab' tanks, 36
Sicily, invasion of, 12, 16
Singapore, surrender of, 8, 16
Stalingrad, Battle of, 7, 11, 16
Stormovik, 7
Stuka, 7
Sturmgeschutz guns, 37
submarines, 10, 11, 28
supply lines, 25
Swordfish biplane, 28, 29

T-34 tanks, 6, 7
tanks, 4, 5, 6, 7, 36, 37
Taranto, raid on, 29
Tarawara, capture of, 15, 16
Thompson submachine-gun, 9
Tiger, 7
timechart, 16
torpedoes, 11
tracks, tank, 6
transport planes, 25

U-boats, 10, 11
    Type VII, 11

V (Vengeance) weapons, 12
V-1 rocket, 13, 32
V-2 rocket, 12, 13
von Braun, Wernher, 12

Wespe howitzer, 37
World War I, 4, 8, 10

Yak 9, 7
Yugoslavia, invasion of, 4